P9-CTP-076

THE PRINCETON REVIEW

COLLEGE
COMPANION

BOOKS IN THE PRINCETON REVIEW SERIES

Cracking the ACT
Cracking the ACT with Sample Tests
  on CD Rom
Cracking the GED
Cracking the GMAT
Cracking the GMAT with Sample Tests
  on Computer Disk
Cracking the GRE
Cracking the GRE with Sample Tests
  on Computer Disk
Cracking the GRE Psychology Subject Test
Cracking the LSAT
Cracking the LSAT with Sample Tests
  on Computer Disk
Cracking the LSAT with Sample Tests
  on CD-Rom
Cracking the SAT and PSAT
Cracking the SAT and PSAT with Sample
  Tests on Computer Disk
Cracking the SAT and PSAT with Sample
  Tests on CD-Rom
Cracking the SAT II: Biology Subject Test
Cracking the SAT II: Chemistry Subject Test
Cracking the SAT II: English Subject Tests
Cracking the SAT II: French Subject Test
Cracking the SAT II: History Subject Tests
Cracking the SAT II: Math Subject Tests
Cracking the SAT II: Physics Subject Test
Cracking the SAT II: Spanish Subject Test
Cracking the TOEFL with Audiocassette
Flowers & Silver MCAT
Flowers Annotated MCAT
Flowers Annotated MCATs with Sample
  Tests on Computer Disk
Flowers Annotated MCATs with Sample
  Tests on CD-Rom

Culturescope Grade School Edition
Culturescope High School Edition
Culturescope College Edition

SAT Math Workout
SAT Verbal Workout

Don't Be a Chump!
How to Survive Without Your Parents'
  Money
Speak Now!
Trashproof Resumes

Grammar Smart
Math Smart
Reading Smart
Study Smart
Word Smart: Building an Educated
  Vocabulary
Word Smart II: How to Build a More
  Educated Vocabulary
Word Smart Executive
Word Smart Genius
Writing Smart

Grammar Smart Junior
Math Smart Junior
Word Smart Junior
Writing Smart Junior

Business School Companion
College Companion
Law School Companion
Medical School Companion

Student Access Guide to America's
  Top Internships
Student Access Guide to College
  Admissions
Student Access Guide to the Best
  Business Schools
Student Access Guide to the Best
  Law Schools
Student Access Guide to the Best
  Medical Schools
Student Access Guide to the Best
  309 Colleges
Student Access Guide to Paying for College
Student Access Guide to Visiting College
  Campuses
Student Access Guide: The Big Book
  of Colleges
Student Access Guide: The Internship Bible
Student Advantage Guide to Summer
Hillel Guide to Jewish Life on Campus
The Princeton Review Guide to Your Career

**Also available on cassette from Living
Language**
Grammar Smart
Word Smart
Word Smart II

THE PRINCETON REVIEW

COLLEGE COMPANION

Real Students
True Stories
Good Advice

MELANIE AND JOSEPH C. SPONHOLZ

Random House, Inc.
New York 1996
http://www.randomhouse.com

Princeton Review Publishing, L.L.C.
2315 Broadway, 3rd Floor
New York, NY   10024
E-mail: info@review.com

ISBN 0-679-76905-6

Edited by: Celeste Sollod
Designed by: Illeny Maaza and Meher Khambata

Manufactured in the United States of America on recycled paper

9 8 7 6 5 4 3 2 1

First Edition

Acknowledgments

Thanks to Joseph, who is my life companion; my parents, who gave me common sense and the self-confidence to use it; my sisters Megan and Allison, who I hope read this book, but who will get my advice whether they want it or not; and my grandparents, especially Dorotha, for being the best safety net and support system anyone could ever hope for.

—Melanie Sponholz

To my wonderful wife, without whom no chapter in my life would be worth writing; to Mom, Dad, and Kay, who give me love and support and who are the paradigm for everything I do in life; to my grandparents, Jane, Jack, Kathleen, and Otto, who made all of this possible through hard work, morals, and family; and to three educators, professors, and friends, Robert Kuhlman, John D. Feerick, and Thane Rosenbaum, for making my personal and academic education so enjoyable and rewarding.

—Joseph C. Sponholz

We would both like to thank our friends, including, but not limited to: Sharon Allen, Brittnie Banks, Andrew Feigin, Anita Holm, and Allan Urgent; our art director, Saki Mafundikwa; and our editor, Celeste Sollod. Their invaluable assistance and seeming willingness to deal with our type-A personalities made this book possible. See you all at Kate Kearny's.

Contents

Acknowledgments v

Introduction 1

Chapter 1: **Going, Going, Gone** 5

Chapter 2: **You Are Here** 23

Chapter 3: **Mapping Your Course** 51

Chapter 4: **You've Got Class** 63

Chapter 5: **When the Pressure Is On** 81

Chapter 6: **Papers** 111

Chapter 7: **Having a Life** 121

Chapter 8: **Get A Job** 151

Chapter 9: **To Your Health** 159

In Conclusion 169

About the Authors 171

Introduction

Congratulations! Getting accepted to college is an important accomplishment. You should be proud and excited to enter one of the most interesting, enjoyable, and challenging times of your life. It also means you can dodge "real life" for at least another couple of years. We promise you that we would give our . . . well, you know . . . to go back for another four years!

However, the fact that your college experience will be one of the best in your life doesn't mean that it's a completely free ride. Along with the pros go the cons. That's why we've decided to write this book. You will be faced with many problems and challenges throughout your college experience. How do you live with a roommate? What the heck is a forced curve? How do you choose a major? We hope to help guide you through your first year of college by helping you understand what to look out for, what to avoid and what to savor. From surviving cafeteria food to studying for exams, joining a fraternity to getting a job, we give it to you straight. Plus, we back everything up by telling you about our experiences, our friends' experiences, and the experiences of the thousands of students who have been surveyed by The Princeton Review.

So, you ask, who the heck are we? Good question. No wonder you got in to college. We are Melanie and Joseph C. Sponholz. (That's why our names are on the cover.) Yes, we're married, we met in college, but we're not old and clueless. Let us tell you a little about ourselves.

Melanie went to Drew University, a small liberal arts college in Madison, New Jersey, where she graduated *summa cum laude* (la dee da!) in 1993. Mel was an English major, but she was also active in the theater, appearing as the lead in more than five productions on campus. She was a Resident Assistant in the dorms for two years. When Mel wasn't busy studying or tutoring French, she was drinking cheap champagne. Oh, but that's not all, she also worked her way through school, first as a school bookstore employee, then as an SAT verbal section teacher for The Princeton Review. Finally, Mel worked in publishing for Country Inns Magazine and then for Random House. She enjoys cooking, needlepoint, and women's literature. Ladies and gentlemen . . . Melanie Sponholz.

Joe went to New York University (Go Violets!?), located in the East Village of New York City, and graduated *cum laude* in 1994. Joe was a politics and French major and also studied economics and biology. Joe was a Brother and a two-time pledge master in the oldest continually active fraternity in the United States, Delta Phi. He worked as a site director and SAT verbal section teacher for The Princeton Review. Joe also took time off in college to help run a congressional campaign as Volunteer Coordinator, then worked as a staff assistant to the member's district office. Joe played intramural football, softball, basketball, and soccer while in school, and managed to fit in time to join an on-campus improvisational comedy troupe. "What a man, what a man, what a mighty good man." Yeah, whatever.

The point of telling you all this is that we each bring something different to this book. (And we like to talk about ourselves.) We did incredibly different things and our experiences were diverse. We don't always agree on everything, and later, after your first year, you'll probably disagree with some things we've said too. Hopefully though, you can glean something from our college experiences which will help you prepare for yours.

Ladies and gentleman, that's not all! We also have the nation's foremost college authority on our side. Believe us, these people are good. The Princeton Review (TPR) has years of experience preparing students for entrance exams and working with students once they're in college. Every year, TPR conducts a nationwide student survey in which they ask real, live college students about their college experiences. TPR meticulously compiles the responses to the survey at their New York headquarters. Well, not really, but the responses were in a big box on the floor and they let us raid it! As a result, throughout this book you will see quotes from current college students describing their thoughts on various topics. In essence, you get the benefit of the thousands of students who work with TPR. Not bad for a couple of bucks, huh?

Keep in mind that we aren't trying to meticulously explain every detail of every college experience. Instead, we want to provide you with a game plan, a plan of attack, if you will. We hope we've done that and that you feel comfortable as you begin your first year.

Good luck and enjoy yourself.

CHAPTER 1

Going, Going, Gone

SUMMER ORIENTATION

Summer orientation, usually a three- or four-day session for freshman held over the summer before you start college, is a great way to spend your first days at the school you've chosen. Attendance may be optional at your school, but there are reasons why you should definitely go.

Meet and Greet

You're probably nervous about showing up in the fall and not knowing anyone. If you're having visions (or nightmares) about wandering the campus alone or sitting by yourself in the cafeteria, then fear no more. Summer orientation was created, in part, to make sure that you start the fall of your freshman year with friends. Remember, everyone that comes to orientation is in the same boat you are. Even if they're coming to college with friends from high school, they'll want to meet new people.

From the time you arrive on campus, the orientation counselors are going to do their best to make sure you bond with the rest of your class. This means you get to do fun things like play name games, pass oranges down a line of people using only your chin, and put on skits about alcohol awareness. Sound stupid? Well let us let you in on a little secret: The orientation staff knows this stuff is embarrassing. How better to get you all talking than to make everyone feel like idiots together? Even complaining about having to think of one more adjective that starts with the same letter as your first name counts as a conversation. So be a sport. You only get out of orientation what you put into it. If you don't participate, a) you'll be really bored and b) everyone will think you're really boring. Don't worry, there will be things to do that you'll actually enjoy. And there will be plenty of time for just hanging out, once you realize that you actually have people to hang out with.

You'll probably end up becoming close to a handful of people over the course of orientation. After all, it's a pretty intense bonding experience. These may end up being some of your best friends for the next four years. Or they may not. What's important is that you return in the fall to some friendly and familiar faces. Remember, you're going to meet a lot more people once school starts, people with whom you have more in common than the fact that you attended the same orientation. For this very reason, you shouldn't feel pressured to find a roommate at orientation. You may or may not find someone who you think would be great to live with. Keep in mind that it's a lot easier to get along with someone for three to five days of fun, games, and all-night conversations than it is to spend a year of real life with them. You probably have just as good a chance of getting a perfect roommate by letting the school match you up with one. (By the way, there is no such thing as a perfect roommate, but we'll talk about that later.)

Make Yourself at Home

Orientation is also your chance to do all of your getting lost and looking like a clueless freshman (okay, you may do some more of this later, too) before the other three classes arrive. Activities are usually organized at lots of different locations on campus, so you get some navigating experience. You find your way to the various classroom buildings, see where the faculty and administrative offices are, get a feel for living in the residence halls, and eat a bunch of meals in the cafeteria. Coming to school in the fall knowing your way around makes a world of difference. Make sure you note the locations of a few offices that will probably be important in your first days at school: the registrar's office, the bursar's office, and the financial aid office.

Most schools have a few residence halls that are used as freshmen housing. Chances are you'll stay in one of them during orientation, but if you don't, make sure you take a look. This is your opportunity to check out your future abode. You may be shocked by the size of the rooms, especially when you think about sharing one with one or two other people. Keep a mental picture of this space in mind, and remind yourself of it before you decide to rent a U-Haul to bring your stuff to school.

Get to Know the OC Team

Getting to know the orientation counselors is a good idea for a couple of reasons. First of all, the students who want to work at orientation are usually pretty cool. There's competition to get on most OC teams, so you get the cream of the crop. Second, these people know your school. They probably play an active role in campus life, and are a great resource. They can help you pick out your fall classes, tell you which professors' classes you should take (and not take), give you an insider's view of Greek organizations and various clubs and extracurricular activities, give you suggestions for jobs on campus, and more. And this usefulness won't end with orientation. It's a good idea to get to know upperclassmen, because they're good for everything from tutoring to buying beer later on.

Summer Registration

You will probably register for your fall classes during summer orientation, or at some other point during the summer. As mentioned above, the orientation counselors are a good source of advice. You'll find our registration tips in chapter 3.

GEARING UP TO GO

Choosing Your Home

Most schools ask you to list your dormitory preferences. There are several factors that determine where you want to live. Do you want to live in a single-sex or coed residence hall? If you want coed, do you want coed by floor or by room? Would you rather be in an all-freshmen or mixed-class dorm? Some schools also offer floors designated as "quiet" or "substance free." Theme dormitories or houses, such as a French House, International Students Residence Hall, or African American House, may also be offered. You know better than anyone else where you'll feel most at home, but, true to form, we'll tell you what we would pick and why.

In case you haven't noticed, the world is coed, and living in a coed dorm gives you good experience in dealing with the opposite sex. In college, probably more than in high school, the social scene is definitely coed. (For some reason, single-sex parties aren't usually the biggest hits.) Even if you already have a boyfriend or girlfriend, you should make an effort to make friends with members of both sexes. If you don't have a boyfriend or girlfriend, do we really have to explain the advantages of coed dorms? What about advantages of single-sex dorms? Well, you don't have to worry quite as much about what you look like when you walk down the hall. Rumor also has it that all-female dorms tend to be quieter and cleaner (we probably shouldn't spread such bald-faced lies). You may find that living in a dorm that's coed by floor is a nice compromise.

All-freshmen dorms are another good idea. It can't hurt your social life to move into a place where everyone is trying to make new friends. It also increases your chances of living with people who are taking the same classes that you are, which means you have instant study groups in the floor lounges and plenty of people to brainstorm with about projects and papers. The plusses of mixed-class dorms include nicer buildings, better parties, and meeting upperclassmen. However, you can enjoy the benefits of these dorms without actually living in them, and, even if you list them as your first choice, you probably won't get into them.

Quiet floors, as far as we're concerned, are pretty useless. Except for weekend nights, dorms aren't usually too loud for you to work in. Remember, everyone else has work to do too. If you need absolute quiet for studying, there are plenty of places, from the library to lounges in classroom buildings, where you can go. You may find you get more done in the library anyway, because dorms offer friends, phones, and many other procrastination aids. Besides, while quiet floors are a nice idea, it would take a quiet building to create real noise-control.

Substance-free floors are unrealistic. You always have a right to live in a place that is free from illegal drug use. You don't have to live with a roommate or put up with a neighbor who is constantly smoking pot or taking acid. (Read about roommates and Resident Assistants in chapter 2 for more advice about this.) Alcohol, on the other hand, is something you will probably have to deal with your whole life, so you may as well get used to it now. Unless you plan on going nowhere but the substance-free floor, which will be difficult once you've graduated, you will encounter drinking. Now is a good time for you to learn either how to say no or, more realistically, how to drink responsibly.

You may want to live in a theme house or dormitory, but we suggest waiting until after your first year. Gain some experience living with a diverse group of people before you decide to move in with a more narrowly defined community. You may develop new interests during your first semester, for instance in a foreign language, international studies, or theater, and decide that you want to live in a house that you wouldn't have considered before. Most theme residences ask you to participate in special programming, such as organizing open houses and other campus events. Language houses will almost certainly ask that you speak only that language while in the house. These living situations can be great learning experiences, but you may want to save taking on the responsibilities they can entail until you've gotten the knack of college life.

No matter what kind of housing you request, or whether or not you get your first choice, you should be psyched about living on campus. Don't worry too much about your decision. Even if you love your dorm, as you make friends you'll find that you have plenty of places to spend your time.

Getting In Touch With Your Roommate

Picture this: You arrive at your dorm room only to meet your roommate and find that you've both brought televisions, VCRs, phones, refrigerators, and perhaps even microwaves (despite the fact that most schools prohibit their use). Not only is there not enough room in your less-than-palatial suite, but even if you could get all this stuff in, there wouldn't be enough outlets available to run it!

Ahh, but don't despair. There is a simple solution to all of this. You call your roommate before you get to school. Keep in mind that this is a somewhat awkward experience for both of you. Not often does one make or receive calls from a total stranger. However, don't be shy. Call and introduce yourself. You'll probably discuss who you are, what you like, and what you each have to bring. The fact is that your roommate is likely to be just as excited, nervous, and anxious to go to school as you are.

What to Pack and What to Leave at Home

You should not be entertaining the thought of renting an eighteen-wheel tractor trailer to bring your possessions to school. Similarly, if you're thinking that you can make it through school with a pair of jeans, your Bob Marley memorial T-shirt and your toothbrush, you're mistaken.

So what do you bring? Well, for starters you have to understand that space is at a premium. Most dorm rooms have only one small closet and one two-drawer dresser for each person. In terms of your clothes then, it's important to pack realistically. Since most students return home at least one or two times, packing seasonally is a good way to do this. Pack your summer and light fall stuff and bring it with you to school first. At Thanksgiving, you can bring these clothes home and pick up your heavy fall and winter stuff. That should hold you until spring break when you take your spring and summer clothes back to school again.

As we said above, you need to call your roommate to divide up what you'll bring. In large part this will be dictated by what you have. However, we have some small hints. Bring the larger stereo. Yes, that's right, the larger. First, you can use the speakers as a coffee table. Second, a large part of social life revolves around music in college. You'll be able to rock the dorm. Finally, your stereo is a defensive weapon. Yes, we're serious. Your next-door neighbor dribbles a basketball at 5 a.m.? No problem, a little one hundred decibel Hendrix at midnight should drown him out or get him to quiet down. Of course, this may not make you the most well-liked person in the dorm.

You should also bring the larger refrigerator. Stores sell one that looks like a four-foot-high rectangle. The cube ones are too small! Some schools will offer to rent you a cube. For the price of renting one for four years you might as well buy the rectangle. Admittedly, the downside is you've got to haul the thing around or put it in storage. You need the bigger refrigerator for lots of things including storing the ice cream, keeping bottled water, and keeping your biology experiment alive. Joe also claims that the bigger refrigerator can be stacked with upwards of two cases of soda (read: cheap beer). One little bit of hopefully unnecessary advice here: Don't try to expedite your refrigerator's defrosting by scraping it with a knife. This is how

Joe found out that refrigerators contain the cooling agent Freon, which leaks out if the side of the refrigerator is punctured, thus making it a useless box.

Handy Things to Have Around That You May Not Have Thought of

- Power strip and extension cords. There are never enough outlets in dorm rooms.

- Fan. If your dorm isn't air-conditioned, you will definitely need one.

- Corkscrew and bottle opener. Obviously only for opening bottles of sparkling cider and root beer.

- Hammer and screwdriver. Not only will you probably need these while you're setting up your room, but you'll meet lots of new people when everyone stops by to borrow them.

- Bathrobe. Unless you want to get completely dressed every time you have to walk down the hall to the bathroom.

- Flip-flops. Standing on the wet (sometimes slimy) floors in the showers and bathrooms can be disgusting without them. Your feet will thank you.

- Shower caddy. Who knew how many things you'd have to carry back and forth to the bathroom?

You should leave home your pet rock collection, your life size replica of Hammurabi's code (you'll learn what it is in Poli Sci 101), and your pet ostrich. Seriously though, you get the picture. Don't bring anything unnecessary. Does that mean don't bring anything that doesn't serve some immediate purpose? No, there is always room for some things which reflect your character and that you feel are important (your velvet Elvis wall hanging, for instance). Your school may even provide some storage space for things like your bicycle, golf clubs, and skis. Call ahead and find out!

Thoughts on Buying a Computer

If you don't have one yet, welcome to the twentieth century. Buy one. That's it. Next chapter. Honestly though, in today's computer age it is absolutely imperative that you have a computer. Consider a computer part of your tuition expense.

If you absolutely cannot afford to buy one, most schools have a computer center available to students. The labs typically have a litany of problems, such as varying hours, incompatible software, and long waits at crunch time. Nonetheless, you won't be dead in the water if a personal computer purchase is simply not an option.

Professors will hand out disks with material you need to know, all your papers will have to be typewritten and on disk as well as hard copy, and you will need to do on-line research. Also, these days you don't call anyone on campus anymore, you electronic mail (e-mail) them. You'll get everything from your professor's course outline to an update on your friend at another college on your e-mail account.

You need to decide what kind of computer to get. Laptop or desktop? How much memory? CD-ROM? We don't know. We're not computer experts. We can tell you, however, that you don't want to be stuck with one that is slow or freezes up on you. So you save a couple hundred bucks by not buying enough memory? Talk to me when your twenty-five-page term paper that counts for 90 percent of your English grade is erased by your machine. What we're saying here is go somewhere where there are computer experts and for the extra cash get one that won't let you down.

Some guidelines for you to take into the store with you are appropriate. First, you want a computer with at least eight megs of memory. Windows 95 won't even run on a computer with less than this. By the work of the computer gods, megs somehow translate into speed. When you've got your modem running, you're in WordPerfect and you're receiving a fax, you'll be happy your computer has enough megs.

Second, make sure you get a decent operating system. For most of the world this means Microsoft Windows or Windows 95. Bill Gates is such a genius that he's somehow figured out how to get the world addicted to this technology. Any computer without it is basically a big black box. (This has been a paid announcement for the Microsoft Corporation. Any reproduction or transmission of the above without the express written consent of Bill Gates is prohibited. Yeah, right.)

Third, you need to get a good word processing program. For the most part, this is what you'll be working with when you use your computer. People have different opinions on what the best one of these is. Some students swear that Microsoft Word saved them in college. For our part, we always used WordPerfect, and in fact, wrote this book with it. Truthfully, it doesn't matter which one of these you use because once you get accustomed to one or the other they're equally effective. Just make sure that you don't get a word processing program that isn't compatible with these. Otherwise, you'll find yourself unable to put the majority of information available to you on your computer's hard drive.

Fourth, you should purchase a modem. A modem allows you to access other computers and data bases through the telephone lines. True, this is not an absolute requirement for your computer, especially if you're trying to save money. However, in order to have access to the now-famous Internet and subscription services such as America Online and CompuServe, you need a modem. Modems operate at different speeds called "baud rates." Most information these days is sent out at least at 14,400 baud, and oftentimes at much higher speeds. Now, of course, the price of the modem is directly proportional to its speed. Nonetheless, don't waste your money on a piece of equipment that will quickly be useless to you. You should purchase a modem that can handle, at least, a 14,400 baud rate.

Fifth and finally, you should consider purchasing a CD-ROM drive. A CD-ROM looks just like a music CD (in fact, you can play music CDs in your CD-ROM drive), but is capable of storing immense amounts of information. This is definitely not a must. However, there are very useful encyclopedias, dictionaries, and other databases that are now available on CD-ROM. You'll be able to use these while you're in school and after you graduate. There are also some pretty cool games.

Getting All That Stuff to School

We've already discussed how much you can take, now we need to talk about how to get it there. In large part, this depends on how far from home you're going to school.

If you're flying to school there will be a limit on the number of bags you can take. You know, "your carry-on luggage must be able to be stowed in the overhead bin or underneath the seat in front of you, blah, blah, blah." You can, however, pay most airlines an extra freight charge to be allowed to take more than the normally required amount of bags.

Perhaps a better, more convenient way to go is to ship some of your belongings to school before you go. The U.S. Postal Service will ship things and hold them at the post office until you pick them up when you arrive on campus. If your school will sign for and hold packages for you, consider using one of the major freight shippers such as Federal Express or United Parcel Service. Obviously, all of this costs money, but the headaches you'll save by not having to carry all of your belongings may well be worth it.

Finally, if you do want to bring everything with you on your first day, you have several options. One is to pack it all in your car. (See the next section on keeping your car on campus.) The drawback to packing up your car is typically that there won't be enough space for you, your belongings and, perhaps, your family. You might also consider renting a truck. Many a student has gotten to college this way. The problems are that to rent a car or truck from most companies, you have to be at least twenty-five years old, and you have to find somewhere to drop off the truck once you arrive at school. You might have to find someone willing to do a round trip U-Haul drive to get you to school.

Can You and Should You Take Your Car?

Deciding whether to bring your car to school will likely be influenced by your college's restrictions on cars on campus. Many smaller schools do not allow freshmen to have a car on campus because of parking space limitations and a desire to foster a campus environment during the first year. Put simply, many colleges feel that if they trap you on campus, you'll assimilate into campus life. Truth be told, it's not a bad strategy. These smaller schools will generally make exceptions for hardship cases, if you need to drive to your job in order to pay for school, for instance. Larger colleges are generally less concerned about space and togetherness and may not have any restrictions at all.

The one constant with all colleges that allow parking seems to be that student drivers register their cars with the school. This requirement serves two functions. First, this allows the school to monitor on-campus traffic. By forcing students to register their cars, campus security can help keep the campus secure from unwanted visitors. Also, when you've parked on the lawn to unload the keg, or parked in the Dean's spot, campus security can write you a nice, hefty ticket. Good luck on getting your grades released if you don't pay it! Second, since schools usually charge a registration fee, it's a nice source of income for campus security.

If your school allows freshmen to have cars on campus, there are certainly benefits to doing so. These include easier access to the malls, grocery stores, and movie theaters. Having a car allows you flexibility in driving to your home or the homes of your friends. Most importantly, you can road trip! Ever start driving to Disney World at 2 a.m., or to New York City for Saturday night? You'll be able to if you have your car. Having a car on campus allows you increased access to the world outside your campus.

But there are drawbacks to having a car on campus too. To begin with, having it may make you the student body's errand runner. It will be difficult to say no to your friends when they want you to take them out, regardless of your exam the next morning. Moreover, as you undoubtedly already know, driving costs money. Everyone always says they'll chip in for gas, though they rarely do, and you'll still have to pay for your insurance and maintenance. You're also going to have to find something to do with your car when you're not driving it. In many areas, such as Boston, New York, and Los Angeles, car parking costs are considerable. Finally, remember that your car may be on campus for holidays, weekends, and vacations, even if you're not. Your school may not be as accommodating as you might think about allowing you to leave your car parked on campus during these times.

Overall though, we recommend bringing your car to campus if your school allows it and you can afford it. You and your friends will enjoy the flexibility it brings during the school year.

THE BOTTOM LINE

Setting Up a Checking Account

Many people have had a savings account since they were children, patiently putting away their pennies for when they wanted to go to college. That's a wonderful image. Practically speaking though, it's time to take the $243.71 you've saved and put it in a checking account. You need a checking account for two main purposes: 1) so you can get a cash card that allows you to take money out of a cash machine virtually anywhere in the world; and 2) so you can write checks.

In order to get a better picture of the banking landscape for college students, we talked to some experts in New York City's financial services industry. These experts informed us that due to the rapidly changing nature of the banking industry in the United States, there is no "rule of thumb" for determining where you should open a checking account. However, they did suggest that students consider two key points when comparing banks. First, you should consider the "total cost" of having a checking account at a particular bank. In other words, having a checking account is going to cost you some money in the form of: 1) checking fees for each check you write; 2) ATM (automated teller machine) fees for each time you withdraw cash; 3) other miscellaneous fees, such as the fee for a returned (bounced) check, or overdraft protection; and 4) penalty fees for having less than a specified minimum balance. Because there are so many banks, you should shop around for the best rates (even try surfing the Net!). You may be able to minimize these fees through agreements personally made with your bank. Talk to your account representative. Tell them you plan on being a customer of the bank for at least the next four years. Tell them you're a struggling student, and ask if they might be willing to waive some of the account fees for a period of time. This may not always work, but it's worth a try. You should also look for special offers made by banks to students at your school. Many schools may inadvertently help you avoid fees. For example, if your school's bookstore will let you cash checks everyday for a certain amount, you won't rack up any ATM fees.

Second, the experts say students should consider how they are going to use their checking accounts. For example, if you are working at a local store to get money for those 3 a.m. pizzas you keep sucking down, you might want a local bank so that your checks clear quickly.

Conversely, if your parents are in a position to help you with your monthly bills, and are going to be depositing money into your account, you may want a larger bank with branches in both your hometown and your college town. So when you've been eating mashed potatoes for six days because your cash ran out on the twentieth of the month, your parents can immediately (after they let you sweat it out a bit) get you cash. Also, you should consider where you're going to be when you're not at school. Having a local bank in Nebraska is going to be a major pain if you're planning on working in Atlanta during the summer.

There are more banking options available to students today than at any time in the past. Local banks have traditionally attracted many college students because, as smaller institutions, a large part of their business is based on individual clients (instead of businesses). These local banks may be more willing to work with students in minimizing fees and structuring a banking plan in order to attract a large college clientele. Larger banks are often attractive to students because they offer the convenience of statewide access and diverse services. However, the experts point out that recently there has been an emergence of "national banks." Such banks include Bank of America, BankOne, and Nations Bank. These banks have taken advantage of the changes in banking regulations and now have branches in small towns and big cities alike. Moreover, they may offer many students the benefits of both a large and a small bank.

As a final note regarding your initial dive into the world of banking, our experts agree that it's impossible to make a "wrong" decision. These are not life and death questions, especially given the fact that if you are unhappy with your initial choices, you can change banks. So don't stress. You might even consider asking your parents for some advice. They've been here before.

Plastic, My Friend. Plastic.

While discussing banking with our financial friends, we thought we'd get you some more free advice regarding credit cards. Heck, they were buying dinner, why not? The experts' advice regarding credit cards was simple: Don't get them if you can at all avoid it. Their opinion was that most first-year students should get used to financial independence on a cash basis. In effect, since most students are on a set budget, whether it's from Mom and Dad, their work income, or their student loans, our experts agree that credit cards, which are often treated like free money, are dangerous.

One thing the experts agree on is that credit cards should only be used as a transactional vehicle or debit card, not as a source of consumer borrowing. Translated back to English, this means that if you have your heart set on having a credit card, you should only use it to purchase what you can pay for at the end of each month. You should never keep a balance on your credit card. The reason is simple: when you keep a balance on your credit card you're essentially borrowing money at an obscene interest rate. The experts feel that many young people miss the point that keeping a balance on a credit card is exactly the same as going into a bank and signing a loan agreement. The only difference is that borrowing money by using your credit card is a lot more expensive. If you have to use your credit card as a way to borrow money, you should only do so as a last resort.

With the understanding that they advise against using a credit card as a way to borrow money, we asked the experts if there was a way to avoid excessive interest charges. They said that it's very important to shop carefully for a credit card, rather than sign the first agreement that appears in your school mailbox, because credit card companies are now offering low interest agreements in order to attract new customers. The experts suggest shopping around on the Internet to see which banks will offer you the lowest rate. You should also discuss credit card fees with the banks that come on campus. Because these banks may make students a large part of their clientele, they may offer a good deal on credit card interest rates.

Finally, make sure you're getting something from your credit card company. These days credit card companies are concerned with the "value proposition" to their customers. Put simply, banks are competing with lower interest rates and "giveaways" to draw customers. You should look to get free airplane miles, telephone minutes, or gas credits. Such incentive programs should be a bonus for lots of college students.

We'd like to thank our experts, who asked to remain anonymous, for their time helping us prepare the information above. They could explain astrophysics to a Labrador. (Kind of like explaining banking and finance to the authors!)

Make Sure Everything Is Square
With the Bursar

The college bursar's office is in charge of making sure that all of the students' bills are paid. This primarily means your tuition bills, but may also include campus telephone bills, campus parking tickets, dorm room fines for damages or misuse, and campus food bills. If you tell the bursar's office that the check's in the mail, they will tell you that so are your grades and course selections for next semester. Learn this lesson now: Don't annoy the bursar.

This however, does not mean that the bursar's office never makes mistakes. In fact, they make mistakes all the time. For this reason, it is important to call and make sure that everything regarding your account is taken care of. This includes making sure that the bursar's office received your signed tuition check (loan or otherwise) and that you are cleared to register for classes. This seems simple enough, but it always gets screwed up. Keep a file of everything you receive from the bursar's office and copies of everything you submit. If there's ever a disagreement about what's been paid, you'll want evidence to back you up.

If you find out that you are on the bursar's hit list, don't panic! It's probably one of the simple glitches that periodically plague college students. Since you will have read this chapter, you'll know to save all your documentation from the bursar's office and to make copies of everything you send them. Let us assure you that the piece of paper which you thought listed the bursar's office hours will probably acquire great significance when you have to prove whether you paid your phone bill. When the man in the bursar's office looks down at his computer screen and smugly says, "Well, we only send the letter about our office hours to people who paid their telephone bill. Since you didn't get the letter, we must be right," you can think of our advice and produce the office hour letter as a proof of payment. We don't know why it works this way, it just does.

DEALING WITH DEPARTURE

Filling out applications, waiting for the mail to come, telling the six million people who have asked you (so it seems when you don't know the answer yet) where you're going to school, packing, talking to your new roommate, packing, registering, packing . . . this has been your college experience thus far. And even with all of this going on, chances are it hasn't felt like you're really going anywhere. Believe it or not, all of the getting ready is almost done. The day will soon come when you get in the car (if you fit, after you've jammed all of your stuff in there), or get on that plane, and actually go!

Dealing with Your Parents' Dealing with Your Leaving

You may be able to tell that your departure day is fast approaching by the strange way your parents start acting. Does your mom burst into tears when you say you won't be home for dinner one night? Does your dad, who seemed to have finally stopped directing your social life, suddenly tell you to be in by 9:30? Or, conversely, do your parents abruptly stop giving you any directions at all? These are signs that your parents are experiencing early withdrawal from their little baby. They may reassert their authority, just to assure themselves that even if the rest of the world is ready to let you out on your own, they are still your parents. Or they may decide that you need an independence wake-up call. It probably doesn't matter if you're the first, last, middle, or only child; your parents can't believe you could be grown up enough to be leaving home. Try to be understanding. After all, they did put up with you for eighteen years (and let's be honest, there was probably a lot to put up with). And, whether you think so or not, you're going to need them even when you're "on your own." There are times when you really want to talk to someone who loves you unconditionally. If they really start to drive you crazy, remind yourself that you only have to put up with it for another few weeks. Then you're outta there!

A little reassurance may help your parents through this separation anxiety. Saying things like, "I can't wait to get out of here," is probably not such a great idea. If that's what you really think, you might consider keeping it to yourself. On a purely selfish note, care packages might come less frequently if you make your parents think you never want to see them again. Let your folks know you'll be in touch.

Fill them in on your plans for departure. In general, just let them know they'll still be a part of your life. Many people find they develop great new relationships with the 'rents, once they're not under the same roof.

High School Sweethearts

If leaving for school also means parting with a boyfriend or girlfriend, there are a few emotions you're probably experiencing. First, you're probably pretty blue about leaving someone who has held a steady position in your life. Thrown in with that you've got anxiety, whether it's over breaking up or over trying to stay together (equally tough challenges). As if all of that isn't enough, you may be ready to shoot the next person who tells you there's no way the relationship will last, or who tells you that college is all about meeting new people.

We're smart enough not to tell you what to do about your relationship. One thought though: Follow your instincts, and keep an open mind. In other words, if you feel that the relationship you're in is something you're ready to work hard to maintain, by all means, go for it. Just don't cling to that decision like a lifeline if two months into the semester your instincts start to tell you something else. After all, you have to make these decisions before your whole life changes. Know that you'll change, and all of the agonizing you go through can't help you predict the future. We'll talk more about relationships in chapter 2.

Keep in Touch—High School Friends

Saying good-bye to your high school friends is another tough part of leaving for college. These are people you've spent the past four years with, maybe more, and you're used to having them around. Honestly, most people we know have not kept in touch with all of their high school friends. Think about it this way: You're going to make at least as many new friends as you have now, and unless you plan to flunk out after your first semester, you can't spend all of your time keeping up ties with forty people. Don't despair, you will keep in touch with a few people. In fact, you may learn something about your relationships when you realize that there are some people you don't mind losing touch with.

Moving On

Well, that's it. You are ready to go. Move up. Move out. Pretty exciting to be on the verge of a new chapter in your life, isn't it? Enjoy this time, and don't worry too much about what you're leaving behind. The parts of your life that mean the most to you—your family and good friends—aren't going anywhere. And you're about to make lots of new friends, and have lots of new good times. So throw your high school yearbook into your suitcase for when you get nostalgic, and let's go!

CHAPTER 2

You Are Here

FALL ORIENTATION

Fall orientation is important. Your college career has officially begun, and orientation helps you ease into your new life. Once again we ask that you look beyond the silly name games to see the true purpose of these first days at school.

Meet and Greet II

Most schools have a couple of summer orientation sessions, so fall orientation is the first time you meet the whole freshman class. Remember back in June, when the orientation committee requested a picture of you? Well, you better hope you sent in a good one, because it's going to be in the book that all of the freshmen get when they arrive. If you're mortified right now thinking of that particular snapshot, don't worry too much. The feeding frenzy only lasts a few days (except for the few copies of the pic books that fall into the hands of the upperclass guys, who want to check out the new girls). Seriously though, try to meet as many people as possible. This is the easiest time to make introductions, because, hey, everybody's doing it.

> *"Many students come to school not knowing anyone, wanting to begin adulthood with a clean slate. It's really wonderful."*
>
> —Wittenberg University Student

The social scene at fall orientation is pretty intense. Everyone is eager to form groups of friends and bond with their roommates. There are more upperclass orientation counselors to meet. And sparks definitely fly as people realize that there's a whole new selection of the opposite sex. Everyone has moved into the dorms now. This means that in addition to the parties scheduled by the orientation committee, independent soirees will be happening all over campus. People are staying up all night, hanging out, and hooking up. The combination of sudden freedom, no academic responsibilities, lots of new faces (and other body parts), and sometimes a beer or two or ten, can be explosive. Just remember, it may seem like you're a guest at a five-day blow-out, but in reality you'll still be there a year from now, and so will everyone else. Lots of people will do idiotic things in the excitement of the first week, but you should make an effort not to be one of them. There are many experiences, including finding true love, doing tequila shots, and having a run-in with campus security, that can definitely wait until at least the second week of school.

You may feel the need to establish your whole social life during orientation and immediately after it. You want the same feelings of security that your circle of friends gave you in high school. You want plans for the next five weekends. You want people to eat your meals with. You want the phone to ring. It's easy to feel like you have to make three new best friends, and you have to make them now, but we'll tell you again what we told you when you went to summer orientation: The friends you make now may or may not be the ones who hang in for the long run. Believe us, when you start taking classes and getting involved in activities and organizations on campus, you will find friends who share your interests and even your schedule.

"I have met the most amazing individuals and made the most incredible friends in such a short amount of time."
—Wittenberg University Student

Finally, one other thing you'll probably want to accomplish right away is becoming best friends with your roommate. This may or may not happen, but your roommate is one person who will definitely be around for a while. Fall orientation is your chance to spend time together and start adapting to cohabitating before the semester kicks off. We'll talk all about roommates in the next section of this chapter.

Make Yourself At Home II

If you attended summer orientation, then the opening days in the fall are kind of a review session. Once again, you go to activities all over the campus and make sure you can find your way around. One new wrinkle is that you probably have your fall class schedule, so finding certain buildings takes on new relevance. Do walk-thrus of your daily schedules, so you don't have to pull out that embarrassing map on the first day of class. Figure out how much time you have between classes, and make a game plan for getting back to your room to switch books, check your messages, etc. You want to avoid trying to set the speed record for the mile because you didn't plan ahead and forgot the notebook you need for your next class.

We told you at summer orientation that you should learn where the registrar's, bursar's, and financial aid offices were. Well, now you probably need to visit them. If you have any problems with your schedule or your bills, take advantage of this relatively quiet period, before the other three classes arrive, to straighten things out. It's always a good idea to make friends with the people who work in these offices, because chances are you'll need their help at some point. Getting the classes you want and paying the bills can be two of the biggest headaches at school, so establish some allies now.

"The red tape is awful, but persistence pays off, and there are some smart, terrific administrators who will help you out."

—Southern Methodist University Student

Shop the Bookstore

Ah, your first visit to the bookstore. This is a place where you're going to spend a lot of time and money over the next four years. "Bookstore" is kind of a misnomer, since books probably account for only two or three of your visits every year. Birthday cards, boxer shorts, Doritos, batteries, soda, film, light bulbs, tissues, chocolate,

T-shirts, tapes, extension cords—you name it, you'll buy it at the bookstore. On your first trip, we recommend that you buy notebooks, printer paper, highlighters, pens, and any other note-taking supplies you need, and leave the actual books until after you've attended your first classes. Professors may tell you that certain books are optional (to be used as supplemental texts), or that you can use any edition of a novel, in which case you can look for the cheapest version you can find. Some stores sell used editions of books, and this can save you money. Don't buy a used book that has too many notes or too much highlighting in it. It will distract, and, depending on how good a student the last owner was, confuse you. Keep the bookstore in mind if you're short on cash at the end of the semester. You can sell any of the books you don't want to keep back to the store. You won't get back what you paid for them—in fact you get a pretty small portion of that—but if you're never going to look at that book of aboriginal poetry again, you may as well get a couple of bucks for it.

Many bookstores will also cash checks for a small fee (maybe fifty cents). This can be a good way to get money if there's no cash machine on campus, or if your bank charges a higher fee for using an ATM.

ROOMMATES

Moooooooooooooooooooom . . . My roommate didn't bring soap!!!

It seems that every once in a while we run into someone who has a great story about their best friend whom they met as their roommate their freshman year in college. You know the minute they met they found out that their parents were identical twins separated at birth, they both think that Tito Puente (you'll probably never learn about him) is the most gifted musician to ever grace the earth, and they both consider smoked salmon on Oreo cookies the best pre-game snack. Most people, however, have a slightly different experience.

We don't want to give you the impression that life with a roommate (or roommates) is a wholesale terrible experience. In fact, it's likely that this won't be the case. However, it's important that you understand going into this that simply because two people are put together doesn't mean they're going to be compatible.

Most schools at least make an attempt to match people of similar attributes in the dorm rooms. This attempt usually consists of the school sending out a questionnaire to all the students in the incoming freshman class. Rather than go through all the typically asked questions, let us simply say that our experience is that there is only one that any school actually pays attention to: "Do you smoke?" or "Can you live with a smoker?" Some states have made even this question moot by legislating a ban on smoking in public places, such as a dorm. However, if smoking is allowed, the schools will usually try to insure that non-smokers live with non-smokers.

Notwithstanding the questionnaire, it usually seems like the residence life people took all the resident applications, threw them up in the air, and started picking them up in the pairs or threesomes that eventually become roommates. What we're saying here is that your roommate selection has as much to do with chance as it does with anything else. "So," you ask, "what do I need to know to improve my luck?" Well, as Joe's father is fond of saying, "luck accrues to the well-prepared."

Best Friend: Fact or Fiction?

Everyone who arrives for her first year at college has a certain degree of excitement, anxiety, and energy. The problems generally begin because different people have different degrees of these emotions. As easy as it seems now, and as difficult as it will seem during your first few weeks at school, you have to keep the relationships you'll form in perspective, including the one with your roommate.

For many people, the experience of arriving at school is almost overwhelming. After all, with a few exceptions, going to college is one of the first times in your life that you're not likely to know anyone before you get there. As a result, most everyone is looking for some type of direction. Since the school has assigned everyone a room and a roommate, it's natural that these become the starting focal point of people's college experience. In fact, it's not only natural, it's usually good. No one wants to have to go to the dining hall and sit alone, or try to find their books in the bookstore alone, or, frankly, do anything alone. Having a roommate gives you an instant companion. However, the relationship you form with your roommate, whether good or bad, is likely to change.

> *"One time at a bar, my roommate suddenly pretended to start talking in sign language to me. It took me a second to figure out what was going on; then I realized she was trying to get rid of two creepy guys who were approaching us. It was all I could do to play along instead of completely cracking up. By the way, the technique worked."*
>
> *—Shippensburg University Student*

First, you and your roommate are going to meet other students on campus. Everyone in college brings something different to the table. You're going to find those people who intrigue you, for whatever reason, and want to spend time with them. This means that if you love your roommate, you two can go out and meet other people together and expand your budding circle of friends. If not, be happy your non-roommate friends will have rooms you can escape to.

Second, you and your roommate will begin different courses, with different schedules and different study requirements. The reality is that unlike the first week of fall orientation, whether you like it or not, you and your roommate will have less time to spend together. Keep in mind that it's possible you might like your roommate better when you only have to see each other a couple hours a day. Regardless, your new busy schedules will affect your friendship if, in fact, you are friends, or give you a much needed chance to get the hell away from the psycho with a key to your room.

Third, you and your roommate will get involved in various on-campus activities. Hopefully, the activities offered at your school will be new and interesting. You'll get excited about them and you'll want to spend more time on them than back in your dorm room. Once again, if you're friends, you and your buddy-type roommate can join the glee club together, thus keeping you in constant contact. On the other hand, if you can't stand your assigned companion, you can join the "my roommate is a freak" psychotherapy support group.

> *"My roommate and I stayed up all night so many times, talking about everything under the sun and laughing hysterically."*
>
> **—New York University Student**

> *"My roommate freshman year was so strange. He just wanted to play Nintendo and chat online all of the time."*
>
> **—Drew University Student**

Fourth, and finally, whether you get along or not, you and your roommate will have had enough of each other at some point, and you'll want to have some privacy in your lives. This isn't as harsh a statement as it seems given the fact that you're not exactly going to be in palatial living quarters. Even your best friend gets a little tiresome when you see him twenty-four hours a day, seven days a week. As a result, you will both be looking for places to escape to as your first year rolls on.

To wrap up, if you and your roommate start out as best friends, you can expect that over time and as you adapt to life in college, your friendship will change. You may stay great friends for life (we certainly hope this is the case), but expect that as you both get increasingly involved in on-campus life, your relationship won't remain as strong as it initially was. On the other hand, if you and your roommate despise each other, there are lots of other people and new and interesting things to do on a college campus. You should be able to get involved with other people and activities to make living with your roommate bearable.

Coping With the Difference

Quick quiz: Do you know who the easiest person to live with is? Answer: Yourself. If every college offered each student his own room, we wouldn't even have to talk about this (and your dorm bill would be the same as the cost of a new Porsche). Unfortunately, this is not likely to be an option on your residence life form. Even if it is, freshmen don't have an ice cube's chance in the Sahara of getting a "single." As a result, you are going to have get used to living with at least one other person in the same room.

Part of surviving with a roommate is understanding yourself. You, like everyone else, have particular quirks and idiosyncrasies. If you can identify these unique characteristics, you can save yourself a lot of potential headaches by modifying your behavior. For example, maybe you can't sleep without your Hong Kong Fooey night light, you study while listening to Anthrax, or you can only get going in the morning if you do step aerobics. These are the things that are going to drive your roommate nuts. If you can be considerate enough to temper those actions which may be, shall we say "unusual," you will have taken an important first step in maintaining your relationship with your roommate.

The Importance of Communication

However, even the most considerate people can't control their roommates' actions. Later in this chapter we'll discuss how to identify real problems with your roommate that you need to get outside help with. For now though, we'll focus on problems you can address yourself. Most roommate problems are fairly innocuous, although they can still make you want to rip out their spleens. The key is to remain calm when dealing with your roommate. For example, if your roommate keeps replacing your Elvis Costello disk in your LL Cool J disk case, ask her to stop. If they keep eating your food, tell them to ante up their share of cash for your grocery bill. Most people, recognizing that they've screwed up, will probably sheepishly make excuses and correct the offending behavior.

When you get to school, sit down with your roommate and talk about some ground rules for living together. Don't be a dork about this. Don't hand your roommate a typed list of suggestions before you've even said hello to each other. Sometime during that first week of orientation, before classes have begun, suggest that you grab lunch or dinner together. During the meal, talk about how you both like to live. For example, you might say to your roommate "Amigo, I sleep like a rock, so don't worry about listening to music while you study late at night. But if you don't mind, I like to crack the window at night when it's not frigid, because I like the fresh air." Perhaps more importantly, listen to what your roommate has to say. If she has to take her allergy pill with milk every morning, don't use the milk she keeps in the fridge on your morning cereal. Getting these details out in the open at the outset will help avoid, although probably not eliminate, friction between you and your roommate.

What we're suggesting is that you act like an adult when dealing with your roommate. We are not suggesting that you be a doormat. We'd be lying if we said we'd never slammed a door on our sleeping roommate while leaving in the morning to get the message across that we heard our roommate do the same as they stumbled in the night before. The occasional alarm has been reset in order to make the point that not everyone has an 8:30 a.m. class. You have got to be careful about this stuff though, because it can get out of control quickly. If you want to play hardball, go ahead, but remember your roommate has the key to your room and can forget to give you things like important telephone messages or the cable bill that's under your name.

It's also important that you and your roommate talk about every problem as it occurs. Most problems don't start out as drop down, drag out brawls. Instead, a bunch of silly little problems are left to fester and grow until one or both people can't handle it anymore. That's when one of you will explode because the other ate the Wheaties, or something similarly stupid. The solution is to maintain a dialogue with your roommate. This does not mean that you should be a nitpicker and greet your roommate with a list of grievances every time he or she walks into the room. You're roommates, not parent and child. However, if something really bothers you, and it's not something you can rationally overlook, tell your roommate as soon as possible. Be rational about this and pick an appropriate time for these conversations. For instance, first thing in the morning, last thing at night, and right after your roommate gets a "D" on her Biology exam are not good times. Nonetheless, don't delay in talking things out. This way you'll avoid a bunch of little arguments creating a huge blowout between you and your roommate.

Finally, never complain to someone else about your roommate before you've talked to them directly. Dorms are small places even in the largest universities. Even if people don't know each other directly, everyone knows someone, who knows someone, who knows your roommate. Your griping will get back to your roommate. This will put him on the defensive, and make any hope of having a discussion to resolve your problems difficult, if not futile. You don't want your conversation to go like this: "Look man, you're killing me with that six foot high pile of dirty laundry in the room." "Yeah, I know. John told me that you told Kristin that I was a slob. Kind of tough for me to ask her out on a date now. So deal with the laundry pal, I figure that makes us even." Get the point? Talk to your roommate directly about your problems. If they don't get resolved, then go tank his relationship with "Kristin." Heh, heh, heh.

"People have a funny habit of listening to the rumor mill—word gets around all too quickly and is often distorted in the process."

—**Wheaton College Student**

Real Problems vs. Real Life

There are some problems that are so egregious that you cannot deal with them alone. Case in point: A good friend of ours arrived on campus to find that his roommate was a sophomore who was a drug dealer. That's right, a drug dealer. Not surprisingly, none of the students in his class wanted to room with him, so the administration (who didn't know about his little problem) put him with a freshman. Luckily, this lasted about three weeks before our friend demanded a room change. You should not hesitate to seek assistance in situations like these. We don't think that it's particularly useful to give you a checklist of problems. In fact, part of being an adult is using your judgment and life experience to make decisions like these for yourself. However, there are some more frequent and serious problems which we should make you aware of.

At the outset, you should keep in mind that if your roommate is conducting any type of illegal activity in your dorm room, you're likely to be involved if they get caught. Examples of this type of activity include selling or buying alcohol for minors, selling, buying, or using drugs, and illegal gambling or betting schemes. Even if you're completely innocent in terms of your complicity in these actions, you're going to have an interesting time explaining that to the school. Do you really want to find yourself in the Dean's office trying to explain that even though the phone rang at all hours of the day and night with the caller saying "Pinto says put $100 on Dallas," you had no idea what was going on? Even if you're successful in convincing the Dean of your innocence, which you may not be, you will be labeled for the rest of your college career (maybe even your life) as the person who was involved in that "betting thing." It's just not worth it. You should look at seeking assistance in these cases as covering your ass and protecting yourself. It's the right thing to do.

The next type of common serious problem involves theft. It is an unfortunate reality that many people steal for various reasons: They can't afford what they want; they like the thrill of doing something they know is wrong; it seems so easy to it do and not get caught; they are legitimately sick. Regardless of the reason, theft is a serious problem on college campuses. What we'd really like to advise is what we told Joe's sister this year when she went to school: Don't bring it if you absolutely can't live with losing it. However, we realize that there are some things that are so personally important that you want to have them with you at school. Consequently, our advice is to safeguard them carefully. Your Resident Assistant (See the "Life in a Dorm" section for an explanation of what an R.A. is) may have a safe that you can store things in, or you might consider buying a small safe to bring to your room. And, duh, don't give out the combo to anyone except your parents at home so they can give it to you if you forget it.

If you are a victim of a theft while at school, you need to report it to your R.A. and campus security. Many students feel awkward doing this because they have a sneaking suspicion of who the guilty party is and they are reluctant to see them get in serious trouble. In other words, sometimes it's going to be your friend or your friend's friend that is a thief. We want to make sure you understand that the rationale that makes you say "Jeez they're sick, it's not that big a deal" is crap. When you're the victim of even a minor theft, you need to report it. The thief needs to get help, and if no one ever steps up and has the sense to report it, they're not going to get it. Moreover, if a thief goes unchallenged and uncaught, they're going to keep stealing. Your signed picture of Bozo the Clown may not be a big loss to you, but your friend's grandmother's eighteenth-century brooch will be a big loss to her.

You may also need to seek assistance in dealing with problems that you don't feel comfortable discussing directly with the other person. It often happens that you, as a roommate or friend, will have a unique opportunity to perceive a serious problem affecting another individual. For example, you might be able to see that your roommate is bulimic or has a drinking problem. We know someone who used to drink Jack and Gingers (bourbon and ginger ale) with their Pop Tarts before going to class (Do not do this). These are things that you need to think about reporting to your R.A., or another official who can help the person. Once again, when to report these kinds of incidents is a judgment call that you're going to have to make. Be careful not to make snap judgments about people, but don't hesitate to act when you see that someone needs help.

Finally, you may need to ask someone to help you in dealing with problems of another's personal habits. One graphic and revolting story should illustrate this point. When Mel was an R.A. at Drew University, several residents of the dorm came down and asked her if she could speak to one resident of the building on their behalf. It seems that one female resident had a problem being careful with her "feminine hygiene products" and her undergarments. To wit, she left them out in the bathroom in public view. Ahhhhguuuuhhh. Mel had to go and talk to the woman about this problem. It turned out that she must have grown up in a barn or something, because she was mortified when she found out that other people had noticed her behavior, and never let it happen again.

You don't have to handle every problem that arises during college life alone. Colleges have residence support staff for exactly this reason. When you feel that you legitimately need help in rectifying a serious problem, don't hesitate to go out and get it. Having a living situation that you are happy with, or at the very least you can tolerate, is a necessity. If you go to the residence life office or administration with a problem, and you feel that they don't address your needs, you may have to remind them who's paying who. We're not trying to sound like campus Rambos, but you are paying thousands of dollars a year to live on campus, and that entitles you to a situation you can, in fact, live with.

Welcome to the Jungle: Life in a Dorm

Dorm life means rooms the size of your bathroom at home and bathrooms you share with forty other people. There are 2 a.m. pizza deliveries, noise levels that would put some concert halls to shame, and walls covered with all of the posters that everyone's parents hated. Get ready for all-nighters in the lounge, group paper-writing sessions, sharing everything you own, borrowing things from everyone else, sleeping in bunk beds, fighting over the phone, building lofts, and throwing parties on Monday nights. There will be leftover pizza for breakfast, and Mr. Coffee will be working overtime. You live with your best friends (and their boyfriends and girlfriends) and create some zany memories together.

For better or worse, it's time to live life in a dorm. We're pretty confident that most of the time you'll think it's for the better. Living on campus is an experience you'll be glad you didn't pass up. What better way to spend your first years away from home, than living with a crowd of friends? Yeah, okay, you read earlier that life with your roommate(s) may not always be a bed of roses—but living with anyone has its ups and downs, and at least in the dorm there are always plenty of people besides your roommate to hang out with. Roommates are only one part of life on campus.

You may never have another chance to spend time with such a diverse group of people. You get a big taste of independence, without a big taste of the bills that go with it once you're in the working world. You have a built-in support network of people who are living through the same experiences that you are. Throw in the fact that you can walk anywhere you need to go on campus (making it possible to get up 15 minutes before class and eliminating the need for designated drivers), and you've got a pretty good deal. We almost forgot to mention the best reason for living on campus: You have fun!

This Is My Room?

We said the dorm-life experience is one of the best parts of college. We didn't say that it wouldn't come with some challenges. Even if you shared your room at home with five siblings, you're in for a few surprises when you move into the dorm. The first will come when you arrive at school with a station wagon packed to the gills with stuff, and realize that your room is about the size of the front seat. Oh, and remember, only half to a third of that room is yours. Ah yes, home sweet home . . .

"I grew up right outside Philadelphia, so going to college in cow country was a real shocker. It's hard to get used to opening your dorm room window to the wafting smell of cow manure."

—Shippensburg University Student

At least for your first year, you'll be sharing your space. Forget visions of Laura Ashley showrooms or spacious bachelor pads. Think functional. With two or three busy students living in a twelve-by-fourteen foot space, you're lucky if you can keep it marginally clean. Storage is a problem. Most dorms seem to have been designed under the misguided notion that college students can fit all of their possessions into four three-inch-deep dresser drawers. Maybe if you're lucky, you even have a shelf or two. We've put together a few suggestions to help you make the most of your space:

- Bring your things to school in a sturdy trunk. Not only can you use it for storage, but it can double as a coffee table, nightstand, etc. Just make sure you don't end up with six trunks between you and your roommates.

- Milk crates—cheap and effective. They don't take up much floor space, but four or five of them stacked up can hold a lot of books, sweaters, food, laundry supplies, or whatever else you need a home for.

- Go to Woolworth's and buy some of the cardboard or plastic boxes that fit under beds. These are good for storing things you don't use everyday.

- Buy a hanging shoe rack. You can buy these to hang on your closet door or from your closet bar. Cleaning the shoes off the closet floor means you can stack a few milk crates there.

- Bunk the beds. Bunk beds do suck, but they give you more living space.

- If your school permits them, build a loft. A nice alternative to bunks, lofts get both beds off the floor, so your whole room can be more of a living room.

You might have noticed that the list above includes several mentions of increasing your living space, as opposed to your sleeping space. This is important, because unlike your room at home, which was a bedroom, your dorm room is bedroom, living room, dining room, kitchen, and study rolled into one. Unless you want to sleep, eat, study, and hang out on your bed, it's a good idea to tuck the beds into as little space as possible. Not to mention that spending all of your waking hours on your bed may make it difficult for you to fall asleep there at night. Get a futon or some big pillows for the floor, and leave the bed for sleeping.

One thing besides extra storage space that can make a big difference in your room is lighting. Most dorm rooms have overhead fluorescent lights that rate a big zero on the mood lighting scale. Not only do they make your room look like it should be in an office building, but they can give you a nasty headache if you read under them. For thirty bucks you can get a halogen lamp that gives you just as much light but is far less glaring and can be dimmed. Another good investment is a small headboard or desk light. These small lights can be relationship savers, since they allow one roommate to stay up reading or writing, while the other sleeps in the darkened area of the room.

A refrigerator is another must. We're not suggesting a full sized Frigidaire. You only need a small fridge, and you can probably rent one from one of the companies that go to college campuses at the beginning of each school year. Split the rental cost with your roommate, and you're not talking much money at all. Why do you I need a fridge you ask? In all of the time you spend studying and hanging out in your room, you may get hungry or thirsty. When you're in the middle of writing that paper, sitting there in your ugliest sweat pants, do you think you'll want to walk down to the bookstore (or down the hall for that matter) to get a Coke? No. Better yet, you're writing that paper at two in the morning and you need a peanut butter and jelly sandwich. Good thing your grape jam is chilling in your fridge. You also need a place to store the food from the care packages that you contracted your parents to send a least once a month. Plus, having a fridge saves you from having to fill the bathtub with ice every time you have a few friends over for beers.

One last note: Be careful with the key to your room. Giving it to a friend or significant other is not a good idea. You and your roommate should be the only people with access to your room. Losing your key is an even worse idea. Waiting around for your R.A. or campus security to come open your door is not fun. More important, if you lose your key the lock will have to be changed, and you'll be paying to have it done. Designate one place in your room your key place—maybe you want to put a hook on the wall—and always put your keys there when you're home. Likewise, pick one pocket of your backpack or bag where you put your keys when you go out. This sounds like simplistic advice, but it'll go along way towards preventing loss.

It Takes All Kinds: Living With A Diverse Population

You've got the roommate thing down now, but don't forget, there's a whole dormitory full of other people that you have to live with. Don't think that just because these people don't live in your room you can ignore them. From the four guys who have turned the lounge next to your room into an indoor soccer arena to the girls down the hall who spray enough perfume to give the building's healthiest residents asthma, you'll know you've got company. Some of these people you'll be glad you've met, and some you'll be sorry you can't bury in cement, but all of them will be part of your daily existence.

"This is the most eclectic student body anywhere. You could have an atheist sitting between a Muslim and a born-again Christian, or a skin head beside a homo-sexual. There are morons, brainiacs, and lots of medio-cre intelligences . . . There's a place for everyone."

—James Madison University Student

"One morning, when I stumbled into the bathroom half asleep, I pushed back the shower curtain to find my next door neighbor in there with her boyfriend. I'll spare you the details, but it was one wake-up call I'll never forget."

—Shippensburg University Student

Living with all of these different people can be great. There's no methodology to who's put where in the dorms (at least none that we can figure out), so who you get for a neighbor is a coin toss. The advantage of this is that you have the chance to make friends with people you may never have met under other circumstances. That super-intelligent, really nice guy who's a nuclear physics major may never have crossed your English-major path if he hadn't lived on your floor. He could turn out to be a buddy, and he'll certainly be The Man when you have to take that calculus exam. What better way to meet men than to live next to two guys from the football team? What better way to meet women than to live next to the president of Chi Omega? Having a lot of people around is good for other reasons, too. When your roommate asks politely if you can get out so she can be alone with a significant other, you need somewhere else to hang out. If you run out of quarters while doing laundry at midnight, you'll be up to your ears in wet clothes if you don't know who to borrow change from. All-nighters can almost be a social event when five or ten people camp out in the lounge. Take advantage of the benefits of group living. Be helpful and friendly, and most of the time you'll find you get the same in return.

So what did we mean about wanting to bury people in cement? Unfortunately, what's going on in the room next to, above, or below you can be just as irritating as what goes on in your room. Take, for instance, the guy above you who pumps the base on his stereo and plays *Disco Hits of the '70s* at 2 a.m. on Tuesday night, or the girl next door who has too much Peach Schnapps one night and only makes it as far as your door on her way to the bathroom to throw up. You should expect various people to annoy you at various times. Just don't forget that you (yes, you) can be a real pain in the ass, too. Before you report your neighbor to the R.A. for waking you up with their noise, remember the time that you pounded on their door at 4 a.m. because you had taken your contacts out and thought it was your room. Your neighbors will also get on your nerves for things like playing Dungeons and Dragons in the lounge, leaving their dirty dishes on every surface of the hall kitchen, and flushing the toilet when you're in the shower (nothing like a blast of frigid or boiling water to help you wake up in the morning). Honestly though, these are all things that you can live with. You may think D & D is for freaks, but someone else may think you're the devil incarnate for being a member of the Young Republicans club. When you live with other people, whether it's in a college dorm or your first apartment, you're going to know it. Believe it or not, you'll learn to fall asleep to the sound of other people getting on with their lives. The night that your neighbors are finally quiet, you have a fire drill. It's just the way life works. Buy earplugs.

> *"Freshman year I was a mess—into the party scene in my dorm and having a hard time adjusting. This year I've found a fun crowd who really care about their education more than partying."*
>
> **—University of California at Davis Student**

Don't get too worked up about the little irritations of dorm life. You don't want to be known on the floor as the one who's always telling everyone to "turn it down," and your R.A. isn't on the floor to act as the noise police. However, if someone is really causing you problems—your insomniac neighbor wakes you up every night by turning the TV up loud enough that you're dreaming Coke commercials in full sound and color—you need to do something about it. Your first line of action should be a polite conversation with the offender. Don't be accusatory. The other person may not realize that he's done anything wrong, and you don't want to put him on the defensive. Just explain that you would really appreciate it if he'd lower the volume a little after midnight. In most cases, the problem will be solved.

If, after your polite conversation, your neighbor cranks the sound to twice the original volume, you might want to ask the R.A. to speak with him. And as we discussed earlier in regard to roommates, there may be problems you don't feel comfortable discussing with the other person involved. These are the reasons that your R.A. is around, which makes this the perfect time to talk a little about your Resident Assistant.

Your Resident Assistant

Residence Halls are usually under the direction of a Residence Director, with Residence Assistants on each floor. The titles these folks have may differ from school to school, but the function they perform is the same. They are there to make life in a dorm easier, safer, and hopefully more enjoyable. Unfortunately, R.A.s often get a bad rap, because people think they're just around to report people for things like underage drinking and noise violations. Hear us out, and you may think differently.

Your R.A. is around to make sure that you don't hurt yourself or infringe on others' rights as residents, and drinking can cause problems in both of these areas. If someone gets drunk and decides it would be fun to pull the fire alarm, the R.A. is going to call campus security. If you pass out next to the toilet, your R.A. is going to take you to the infirmary. Before you think that he or she is a jerk for doing these things, think about this: The fire department would be more likely to report the offender to the police. And it may be bad to end up in the infirmary for alcohol poisoning, but it's a lot worse to end up dead because you choked throwing up. It may tick you off when your R.A. tells you to turn down your stereo, but we bet you won't make it a semester before you complain to your R.A. about someone else.

You can avoid conflicts by deciding right now to act responsibly. Drinking underage is illegal, and your R.A. can't do anything about that. But if you drink responsibly—know your limits, don't use alcohol as an excuse to act like an animal, and don't stroll the halls with open bottles—your R.A. will have no reason to report you. The same thing applies to noise. At the floor meeting at the beginning of the year, your R.A. will probably ask everyone to come to a consensus on "quiet hours." You pick a time range, for instance 1 a.m. to 8 a.m., during which everyone is supposed to keep it down. Unless you're making a racket at 1:30 a.m., your R.A. probably won't bother you about noise either. Of course there are a few exceptions. Everyone knows of one R.A. who acts like the dorm dictator and writes people up left and right. But for the most part, reasonable behavior on your part should result in the same from the dorm staff. You should also remember that a lot of the time the reason your R.A. shows up at your door is that your neighbor called and complained about you.

That takes care of the negative aspects of an R.A.'s job. There are many reasons why Resident Assistants are good people to have around. First of all, the residence life staff is connected. During their training they learn about all of the resources your school has to offer, and they know people in every office. No matter what kind of problem you have, your R.A. will know who can help and how you can get in touch with them. This doesn't apply only to problems related to life in the dorm. If you need a tutor, want help writing a resume, or are looking for a job on campus, your R.A. will probably be able to give you good advice.

R.A.s are also great listeners. If you want to talk through a problem, you can go to your R.A. without worrying that it will be broadcast via the grapevine or having to listen to a slew of useless suggestions. This is particularly important when the problem involves your roommate or someone else in your dorm. As we told you earlier, it can be risky to talk to other students about how irritating your roommate is. By the time the story gets back to him he's heard that you called him an ax-murderer. Your R.A., on the other hand, has had plenty of experience dealing with roommate problems and won't mention to your roomie that you'd like to have him transferred to the basement. There are countless sensitive issues, from hygiene problems to kleptomania, that you may encounter during your years in the dorms. Your R.A. has been trained to help you resolve the problems you're not comfortable confronting on your own.

Finally, R.A.s help take care of the building you live in. If the hall light is burned out or there's no hot water, your R.A. gets the right people on the job. So, if you want a quick response when your heat stops working in January, be nice to the res life staff. Actually, being nice to your R.A. is a fine policy in general. They enjoy their jobs most of the time, but no one likes being woken up in the middle of the night to let someone into his room, or telling a room full of partyers to turn it down. So try to take it easy on them when they ask you to come to a floor dinner or tell you that you can't throw a keg party in the lounge.

Getting Involved

If there are things about life in the dorms that you don't like, or you have suggestions for improving the system, get involved. Most schools have a Board of Residence Life, Living Council, or some other student organization that focuses on improving life on campus. These groups meet with the Office of Residence Life and have input when new policies are being instituted or old ones are being changed. They also sponsor and organize activities within the dorms. You can help plan a ski trip for your residence hall, schedule a self-defense seminar, organize a campus-wide picnic, or start an annual food drive.

Regional or national Living Council meetings can also give you a chance to exchange ideas with committees at other schools. Working with one of these committees is a good way to find out if you might like to work on the residence life staff. Being an R.A. is a great learning experience; it can get you free room and board (and a single), and, bonus, it looks great on your resume.

FORGING FRIENDSHIPS

We talked a little bit about forging a relationship with your roommate during the first week of school, but we thought it was also important to discuss the friendships you'll form with others during this same period. As we said before, everyone in college brings something different to the table. Whereas in your high school most of the students were roughly from the same geographical area and background, in college it's likely that the student body will be more diverse. This is one of the very cool things about college.

At first it may seem like you have no friends at school. Quite frankly, it takes time to meet people, and everybody is too busy trying to figure out what's going on to worry about bonding. Don't worry if you feel alone or if you're not particularly comfortable with the people you're hanging out with. This is a natural and common occurrence. Relationships at the beginning of school may be formed more because they are advantageous at the moment, rather than for their long-term prospects. Don't let this upset you. Although it doesn't feel like it at the time, you can't possibly meet and seriously talk to even a fraction of the students on a college campus in the first week. Significantly, neither can anyone else. Similar people with similar interests will meet each other in time. These are the friendships that last.

In that same vein, if you feel that you are perfectly suited to and comfortable with the new friends you've made, you should expect that the group dynamic will change. Just as we said above, the people in your initial circle of friends are going to go out and "meet and greet." As a result, people may want to expand or contract your circle of friends or move on to what feels right for them. Although it may seem hard, don't take these actions as a personal affront, because they're not intended that way. For the first weeks of school understand that friendships are malleable and changing. Keep your head up, and do your own thing, and everything will work out fine.

Different People, Different Ideas, Different Lives

Before we end our discussion on all of the great new things you'll experience, we need to talk about who you'll experience them with.

College has a way of bringing different people with entirely different backgrounds and personal experiences together. Unlike high school, where the majority of students had similar backgrounds because you all came from one or two of the same towns, everybody in college will bring something new and interesting to the table.

What follows from this is that your fellow students will be different from you. They will be different in age, race, religion, political affiliation, sexual orientation, and a million other ways. Moreover, this diversity is good. In real life, people are different. You're going to meet people with whom you completely disagree, but with whom you love to hang out. You'll meet people you think are great but who think you're a moron, and you'll meet people you can't stand and who can't stand you. Not everything is resolved in a half-hour like on television. Nonetheless, it's important that you develop a respect and understanding for your colleagues, as they will provide you with some of the most valuable parts of your education.

For example, when Joe was a freshman in college, he was walking through the University Center when he saw a sign for open auditions for the on-campus improvisational comedy group. He noticed that a couple of his orientation leaders, Mike, Sue, and Deb, were running the auditions. Joe had become friends with these three, and they used to give him a tough time about how conservative he was. Before Joe walked in to the audition, he thought to himself, "Ahh, what the heck, this liberal comedy group is never going to take me, but I should have some fun in the audition." Joe's friends were surprised, and they took every opportunity to bust Joe's chops. Joe fought back. When they'd do a skit making fun of politicians, his troupe-mate would be the Republican, and Joe would be the Democrat. It got nasty, too, but it was all in fun. More importantly, it made for great comedy. Joe made the comedy troupe. The point is, though, that although Joe and his colleagues could never have a serious discussion about where the country should go, they were great friends. That's primarily because everyone respected each other for what they enjoyed in common.

We were recently out with one of our good friends, Alan, and asked him what he remembered from his first-year experience. He said he'd think about it and write it down for us. Although his story occurs later in his first year than orientation, we thought what he gave us was such a valuable perspective on meeting other people that we've included it for you almost verbatim.

Alan, who is African American, began his first year of college at the University of Massachusetts at Lowell in September, 1989. He was a local student, having grown up in Lowell, a working-class Massachusetts city with a small percentage of African American people.

During his first year at Lowell, he met some of the other African American students on campus and was invited to a Black Student Union meeting. He and an African American friend of his decided to go to see what these folks were all about. When Alan and his friend got to the meeting, they found they were the only local students in a room of about twenty people. Most of the students came from larger Massachusetts cities like Boston or Springfield, and a few students had also come from mid-Atlantic states.

Alan told us that he remembers the latter half of the meeting getting abruptly tense when an older woman student started talking about her perception of the white students on campus. Realizing that he and his friend were the new faces, someone asked them if they hung out with white students.

For the next few minutes, Alan argued with someone over whether any of the white students he knew were actually his "friends." "No they're not," a woman sitting across from him said. "You just think they are." "How do you know that?" he replied, "I've known some of these people for years." "They might not say racist things to your face, but that doesn't mean that they're not thinking them. Whatever they may think of you individually doesn't change their perception of black people as a whole. To them you're probably the one black person they like because you don't 'act black.' " "I act the way that I am," he responded.

At that point, another student interjected. She said that it was too bad that Alan had told her that he couldn't attend an upcoming B.S.U. conference because one of the topics was going to focus on race relations on campus.

At that point, someone suggested that the group end the meeting by singing "Lift Every Voice and Sing," a song that is called the Black National Anthem by many African Americans. Alan told us that he had never heard it but was impressed by its words and the feeling that he got realizing that for once he was in a room full of students where he wasn't a minority.

When we asked Alan why he shared his story with us, he said that he relayed his experience at U. Lowell not to analyze the degree of truth or falsity in the argument that he had with his fellow student, but rather to point out that there is no one way that African Americans experience life on a college campus. He thinks that, to a large extent, the quality of anyone's experience depends on his familiarity with the racial and social environment, his personal attitudes toward assimilation and separateness, and his personal decisions about whether to use college as a place to gain exposure to other cultures and ideas.

He went on to say that students of color on predominately white campuses have to handle the universal pressures of adjusting from high school to the college environment, but they must also confront varying degrees of cultural displacement and subtle racism that make the first year of college even more difficult.

In general, Alan thought, race relations on most college campuses are probably not as polarized as the imagined situation in the 1994 movie *Higher Learning*, but the occasional racist remark followed by the aside "no offense" is still very much a reality. Moreover, he said that an organization like a Black or African American Student Union may provide many students a tremendous amount of support, and an opportunity to raise their levels of consciousness on issues of concern to black people. However, members of these groups should also guard against the tendency toward wholesale alienation of entire groups of people. Alan wrapped up his thought by explaining to us that African American students, like all other students, should take advantage of opportunities on campus to increase awareness of their culture, while still retaining the flexibility to learn about the cultures and experiences of other students.

Alan's story has universal applicability. When you get to campus you're going to go through a variety of new experiences and meet a lot of new and different people. Be open-minded, try everything, respect your colleagues, and always be yourself.

OTHER EMOTIONS

There's No Place Like Home

At some point during your first weeks at school, you may wish you could click your heels together and be back home. Your annoying little sister was nothing compared to your roommate. You miss your high school friends. And, don't tell anyone, you even miss your Mommy.

This is a pretty standard reaction. Orientation is jam-packed with activities for a purpose: They keep you too busy to be homesick. However, after the first couple of whirlwind weeks, you have to fill your own schedule. That can be pretty intimidating. Don't feel that because you don't have something to do or someone to be with twenty-four hours a day you're a loser who's never going to get a life. First of all, if you think about it, you didn't have something to do every minute when you were at home. Admit it, you actually spent time alone before college. Second, you're in a little lull between the time when orientation ends and your schedule fills up with new activities. As you get involved with more things, from the school paper to intramural sports, your calendar is going to get crazy. As a matter of fact, you should cherish the space you have now, because in another month you'll be complaining that you don't have enough time to get everything done.

Did that little pep talk work, or are you ready to throw this book down and make another long distance phone call? Before you end up owing your firstborn child to AT&T, we'll try one more tactic: Get off your butt and take some action to make yourself feel better. If you're sitting alone in your room, it's probably not for lack of other opportunities. Go take an aerobics class; sign up to work at your school's radio station; join the French club; just do something! You sure aren't meeting any new friends watching "Oprah."

Oh, and a couple of other things. No matter how tempting it seems, going home every weekend is not going to make you feel better. It may be nice while you're there, but when you get back to campus you feel left out all over again. The first few weekends may be rough, but they're not going to get any easier unless you stay put and make an effort to get involved. We're not saying you shouldn't go home at all; of course you want to see your family.

Just don't make weekends at home a ritual. Likewise, it's okay to call home—the folks would be upset if you didn't—but don't glue your ear to the receiver. Make a deal with yourself that once a day, when the urge to dial hits you, you'll get out of your room and do something else instead. Even if you just walk to the bookstore to buy a soda, chances are you'll run into someone you know and start feeling a little better.

> "The student body is like one big family . . . You know someone wherever you go. I like seeing familiar faces. It helps with homesickness."
>
> —Wheaton College Student

Give yourself some time to feel better. Guaranteed, there are many other students feeling a lot like you do. And don't pick up transfer applications during your first month of school. Getting settled in will be as hard at another school as it is where you are. If it's January and you still feel like you're in the wrong place, maybe then you should discuss your options with Mom and Dad. Betcha that doesn't happen!

Long-Distance Relationships

These first few weeks can also be a rocky road for long-distance relationships. At dinner you may be having a great time with your friends, maybe even noticing how great Mr. or Ms. X is. By nine that night, dinner seems like it was a year ago, and all you can think about is how much you miss that special someone back home. What's going on? Don't worry, you haven't developed a split personality. We're not psychologists, we can only speak from experience, but here's how we'd explain what's going on.

Making new friends is one of the best parts of college. However, it should come as no surprise that it takes some time to get as comfortable with your new friends as you were with the ones you left behind. Sometimes you want to talk to someone who you have some history with, whose relationship to you has the stability that comes from a few years of experience. Chances are your high school boyfriend or girlfriend is one of the few friends from home that you talk to on a regular basis, so those calls feel pretty important. All the homesickness you feel for all of your old friends can get lumped onto what you feel for that one person.

Two more weeks go by, and the fun times are outnumbering the I-just-want-to-go-home times. You seem to be running into Mr. or Ms. X more and more often. You find that you look forward to seeing this other person, and you even hope that he or she gives you a call. Whoa! Does that mean that you don't care about your high school girlfriend or boyfriend anymore? No. It just means that you're in a new place, and you're developing a whole new social life. It's natural that you want to share all this with someone who's right there and can play a part in your daily life.

You may feel guilty about liking someone new, but don't be too hard on yourself. Rarely do people marry someone that they meet in high school. You change and learn a lot about yourself in the first few years in college, and, as you change, so does what you're looking for in a partner. Both of us had high school sweethearts when we came to college, and (obviously) we moved on. We realize that telling you that this is a normal process isn't making you feel any better. So we'll leave you with a few last pieces of advice:

- **Trust your instincts.** This is all about emotions. Your mind may come up with a hundred good reasons why you shouldn't kiss this new person, but your lips are going to listen to your heart.

- **Don't beat yourself up over this.** The reason you don't get married when you're sixteen is that you're *supposed* to change your mind.

- **Be honest.** You're going to feel guilty, and you're not going to want to tell your old flame what's going on. If you really care about them, you'll be honest and let them start moving on, too.

We know from personal experience that that last bit of advice is tough to follow. It's tempting to keep your high school girlfriend or boyfriend hanging on, because you're worried that your new relationship won't work out. Sorry, you can't have it both ways.

And if you think you feel like a jerk breaking up with someone, try facing them when they find out you've been dating someone else behind their back. Enough said.

As If All of This Isn't Enough . . .

We suggest you take a few moments to contemplate all of the information and advice we've just thrown at you about adjusting to your new life on campus. Okay, time's up! Honestly, we hope everything we've written here will be helpful at some point, but how it applies to real life will vary for every single person who reads our book. So, take a deep breath, because there's more! Yes, more. And we're going to move on to the whole business of the college experience: Getting an education.

CHAPTER 3

Mapping Your Course

THE CORE OF YOUR LIFE IN COLLEGE

I've Got To Take WHAT?

How do you feel about "Introduction to Anthropology"? No good? Well, what about "Literature of Third World Islands"? Not that either, huh? Okay then, we're sure you're gonna love "Mendelian Genetics." What we're talking about here are the "core" courses that most schools require you to take in order to graduate. We didn't think we'd take the courses above, but we did to fill our Humanities requirement, our Fine Arts requirement, and our Science requirement, respectively. It's probably an appropriate time to talk about what it takes to graduate.

First things first. Colleges usually require that a student take a specified total amount of classes, a.k.a. the graduation requirements, in order to get a degree. There are several types of undergraduate degrees offered at most colleges: 1) Associate of Arts (A.A.); 2) Associate of Science (A.S.); more commonly, 3) Bachelor of Arts (B.A.); 4) Bachelor of Science (B.S.). The Associate's degrees are completed at most schools after two years of full-time study. The Bachelor's degrees are completed at most schools after four years of full-time study.

Another way schools decide when to award degrees to students is to keep track of their credit hours or credits. To say that you have the necessary amount of credits to graduate is the same as saying you have met the graduation requirements. It works like this: Each course is assigned by the school a certain amount of credit hours necessary to complete it. Most schools are either on a three-credit or four-credit per course system. As a result, you will have to attend class either three or four hours per week in order to complete the course. You will need about 120 credits to graduate. This usually breaks down to an average of five courses a semester at three-credit class schools, for an average of fifteen credits a semester, or four courses a semester at four-credit class schools, for an average of sixteen credits a semester. Do this for two or four years respectively and you'll have your Associate or Bachelor degree.

Your 120 credits will break down into three categories: major requirements, core requirements, and electives. As we mentioned above, everyone has to fulfill the same core requirements. Thus English majors may take "Mendelian Genetics" and political science majors may take "Literature of Third World Islands." The "core" is usually made up of a course or two in every major subject area: English, History, Math/Computer Science, Arts, Religion/Philosophy, Science, Social Sciences, and Languages. You'll probably have to take a few classes that you wouldn't choose on your own, but that's the whole point. Schools want you to get a well-rounded education. Kind of like flossing your teeth, core requirements may not be fun, but they're pretty painless, and they can be good for you. Who knows, that bio class that you dreaded taking may be the first step in your deciding to go to medical school. It may be a small consolation, but you do get some choice of core classes. Although you can't get out of fulfilling your Math/Computer Science requirement, you do get to decide whether you'd rather take Statistics, Calculus, or Computer Programming.

When you declare your major, you'll have another set of requirements. You have to take a series of classes in the area of your major, Art History for example, and usually several classes in related areas, possibly Religion, Languages, or Anthropology. We'll talk about majors in depth later in this chapter.

Finally, you get some electives. Honestly, almost every class you want to take will end up fulfilling some requirement, but you may decide you want to take Pottery I, II, and III, in which case a couple of them will end up as electives.

Keep track of your requirements. We'll probably tell you this several times, but that's because it's important. You need to do a good job of gradually fulfilling your requirements, so you don't end up taking double course loads both semesters your senior year. Now let's get down to the business of registration.

Registration Strategies

Taking your first look at a course catalog can be intimidating. Most schools offer a huge number of classes each semester. How do you know what to choose? You could take all classes that start with the first letter of your name, or close your eyes and randomly put your finger down on the catalog pages, but we don't recommend these tactics. Start with a plan of action. As a freshman, begin browsing through the course selection with several objectives in mind: 1) Take at least one class that fulfills a core requirement; 2) If you have a potential major in mind, try one class in that department; 3) Balance your work load.

Taking a core class or two is a good idea for two reasons. Obviously you want to start getting these courses out of the way, but they can also help you determine your academic direction. If you start out your college years taking a diverse selection of classes, you have a better chance of finding the major that's right for you. There are topics from Art History to Zoology that you've probably never studied before college. For all you know, you're destined to be the next Jacques Cousteau or Henri Matisse. You won't find out unless you try out some new fields. If you already think you could be a Pulitzer Prize winner, now is a good time to take those introductory Journalism classes. This will either confirm your interest and get a couple of your major requirements out of the way, or let you know that you still have some shopping to do before you declare.

Balancing your work load is also important. You've got enough to adjust to first semester freshman year without burying yourself up to your neck in work. Before you dive into extra credits and tough classes, get your feet wet with a standard load of introductory classes. If you want to take a class that looks challenging—Introduction to Genetics—go for it. Just make sure that you balance out your schedule with a couple of classes in areas where you feel more confident. You may also want to consider the kind of work that's likely to be involved in each class you take. You will most likely have to write several papers for an English or History course; a Biology class will involve laboratory work; a Math course may only have exams. Course descriptions in the catalog will give you a good idea of the kind of work that will be required. Choose a variety of formats, so you don't end up writing twelve papers your first semester, or having lab every afternoon.

Cruising the Course Catalog

You've heard the strategies, now it's time to pick your classes. Start with a general idea of what requirements you want to fill. The following would be a good example:

> **Core science requirement:** It's a good idea to get a core course out of the way, and this is a lab course with no papers. You like science, but it's challenging for you: Make sure you don't take other really difficult courses this semester.
>
> **Introductory writing requirement:** Some colleges make you take this before you take any other English courses or upper-level classes.
>
> **History course:** You loved history in high school and think you might want to major in it.
>
> **Core arts requirement:** Another area you have to cover. Your English and history classes will require several papers, so a paper-free art class is a good idea.

If you go to a school with a four-credit system, four classes is a full load. At a school with a three-credit system, you have to pick a fifth class.

Now you can start through the catalog with a sense of direction. Most catalogs are arranged by subject, with courses listed by level within each subject. You can turn directly to your target areas, and check out the introductory courses. This is the fun part, because within those subjects you can pick the courses that look most interesting to you. For your science class alone you may choose between intro courses in astronomy, biology, chemistry, physics, genetics, and oceanography. Take your time, and read all of the descriptions carefully with your objectives in mind. An art history class may look really interesting, but if it requires two fifteen-page papers it might not be a good idea to take it with English and history classes. This is a good time to ask upperclassmen for advice. You may think a Drawing and Painting class looks great, but find out that a few people who have taken it say that they've gotten more excitement from watching grass grow. Conversely, you may have blown right past a course on the Civil War that had a dry description in the catalog, but find out that the professor who teaches it is known as one of the best on campus.

Scheduling

As you pick your classes, you also have to keep timing in mind. If you sign up for one class that meets on Monday from 9 a.m. to 11 a.m., and one that meets on Monday from 10 a.m. to 12 a.m., you're going to have a problem. You also don't want to have seven hours of class in one day. Try to spread your classes out over the course of the week. A good way to go about this is to draw a little table that shows Monday through Friday broken into one-hour blocks. As you pick out potential courses, pencil them into the blocks of time that the class meets. This will let you see at a glance if the classes you're thinking about can work in one schedule. Start out by writing down every course that interests you. Many intro classes are offered at more than one time, and you should write down both times for courses you want. You may end up with three history classes and several classes that meet at the same time. That's fine. After you write everything down, go through and come to the best compromise you can between courses that are your favorites and class times that fit into a reasonable schedule.

Think you're done? Not so fast. Once you come up with your ideal schedule, you have to come up with alternate selections for each class. Depressing as it is, your first choice of class or class time may be full by the time you register. When you're standing in line at the registrar's office, or on the phone in the middle of an automated registration system, you won't have the time to look for alternatives. Write down a contingency plan now, and you'll save yourself a huge headache later.

Registration

After only a week of intense planning, you are finally ready to actually register. There are two typical systems of registering. At many schools you get the pleasure of standing in line at the registrar's office for several hours, with all of the other freshmen. There will probably be a black board, or some other kind of posting, that lets you know when classes are full. You'll see a lot of people panic as classes fill and mess up their entire plan. Not you—you have your contingency plans ready! Anyway, after what seems like an eternity, you'll make it to one of the desks inside, where it will take approximately two minutes for your selections to be entered into the computer system. Tah-dah! You have a schedule. The other option, registering through an automated phone system, can be much more pleasant. You're told which day to call in and given a code number. You just call, type in your code, then follow the computer's instructions as you type in your course numbers. You may have occasional problems with being put on hold or the computer system being down, but overall, you'll probably prefer this to the wasting-your-time-in-line method.

"Although the phone registration process is easy, getting the classes you want as an underclassman is next to impossible."

—New York University Student

What's Your Major

What's a Major?

Yes, it's part of a cliché pick up line that will never work. Yes, it's a question that you will hear and ask over and over again when you are looking for a way to make meaningless conversation. But it's also the focus of much of your college years, a label that people will use to try and identify where your interests lie, and something that you may go on to love or dread. Let us explain.

Essentially, your major is the topic in college that you have chosen to specialize in. Majors are generally associated with the various departments in a college or university, although some majors are completed in several departments. For example, Joe's major in college was "Politics." He had to meet all the requirements set by NYU's Department of Politics in order to graduate with a B.A. in Politics. Mel's major was "English." She had to meet all the requirements of Drew's Department of English in order to graduate with a B.A. in English. One example of a major that crosses over departmental boundaries is "Pre-med." To be a pre-med major at most schools, you have to complete courses offered by the Chemistry Department, Biology Department, Physics Department, and Math Department. Pre-med majors graduate with a B.S. degree, usually in Biology.

One of the great things about college is that there are a variety of courses to take. Unlike high school, where you were assigned the same general topics every year, college will allow you to try a bunch of new things. This also means that you can specialize (major) in a wide range of topics. For example, depending on what your school offers, you can major in Anthropology, Business, Chemistry, Design, Economics, French, German, History, Italian, Journalism, K(C)ooking (we couldn't think of a K major), Latin . . . etcetera. You get the idea.

We talked before about how each school set certain requirements for graduation. The department in which you have your major will have similar requirements. Perhaps the best way to illustrate this is by example. To that end, we're including a sample of the requirements set forth by one college's Politics Department (who shall remain nameless). It reads:

> Welcome to the Politics Department. We are very glad you are majoring (or minoring) in Politics. The following are some essential points about our major:
>
> To major in Politics you must complete at least eight 4-point courses in Politics with a grade of C or better.
>
> Of these, at least two must be chosen from among the four "core" courses that we offer in the fields of political science—political theory, American government, comparative politics, and international politics. At least one course must be taken in three of the four fields.
>
> If at all possible, core courses should be completed by the end of the sophomore year.
>
> Internships and independent Readings and Research courses are recommended but do not count toward the eight courses you have to complete for the major. The exception is the seminar/Internship in Urban Problems in New York City Government.
>
> In general, our major has few specific requirements. This means:
>
> You have to decide for yourself, in consultation with faculty, in which area of political science you want to concentrate, and structure your course selections accordingly. It is generally better to concentrate in an area rather than to take courses "all over."

In this four credit school, you have to complete 32 credits in order to complete your major. The good news is that these credits count toward your overall necessary graduation total. In other words, if you need 120 credits to graduate, your major will account for a quarter of the total. There are also some individuals who, because they love being at the library day and night, "double major." This means that you are attempting to meet the major requirements of two separate departments. This requires an incredible amount of self-discipline and work. Most people don't double major, and as a result, need a whole bunch more credits to fulfill the graduation requirements. Which brings us to . . .

What's a Minor?

A minor is someone under the age of eighteen, who is usually repressed by an all adult society that shamelessly strips the rights of those young Americans who work so hard to maintain the fabric of our . . . Whoa. Sorry. We got carried away a little bit. A minor is really a sub-specialization in college. In almost every respect a minor works the same way as a major.

Just as in your major, there will be requirements set by the department in which you'd like to get your minor. Typically, you will need to take about half the number for credits in your minor that you need to for your major. In other words, at four-credit course schools, you will probably need to take four classes of four credits each in your minor. At three-credit course schools, you'll need to take five three-credit classes. Once again, all of these credits count toward the overall total you need to graduate.

Generally speaking, you can minor in any department that also has a major. Of course, you can't major and minor in the same department. (There is no one out there who was a Economics Major with an Economics Minor.) Also, your major and minor don't necessarily have to have any correlation. For example, it's perfectly fine if you're interested in Theater, but since you want to be able to get a job when you get out, study Business. You can have a Business major with a Theater minor. Melanie, for example, was an English major with a French minor. Now she's a gifted linguist. (So her resumé says.) Well, she's got a good job.

Declaration of Dependence

At some point during your college career, you're going to have to inform your school what you intend to major in. We don't know why. Perhaps the school wants to know your major so that you don't spend your four years listening to reggae and taking freshman studies classes. Or, maybe the school cares because they don't want you to get a degree in "Scheduling Afternoon Classes." Either way, you need to think about what you'll eventually major in.

There are two common mistakes people make in deciding on their major. The first is that many people declare their major at the outset of their freshman year. This is a bad strategy. Ask yourself whether it makes any sense to pick your specialization before you even know what's out there or what interests you. Yes, we are well aware that "major students" are given priority in some classes, such as "Biology 101" for pre-med majors. Keep in mind that there are three classes ahead of you full of people who just declared their pre-med majors because they figured out what M.D.s make a year. Guess who's going to get the priority now? You got it: anyone but you.

We also know that there are some of you out there who always knew they wanted to be anthropologists. In fact, you only went to your school because of the quality of their dry bones collection. Time for a little story. There once was a boy named Joseph who had decided to become a doctor. No question about it: Joe was destined for medicine. He even had his stethoscope picked out before he got to college. Unfortunately, when young Joe couldn't figure out the difference between an isotope and Isotoner gloves, a nice long conversation with his professor discussing his imminent failure of Chemistry 101 quickly disabused him of his medical aspirations. Stop the presses. Rewrite. There once was a boy named Joseph who decided to become a lawyer . . . Get the picture? Joe wanted to be a doctor, but he wasn't any good at the course work needed to become one.

The point is this: You're major isn't going anywhere. You can take your time and survey lots of different classes, even while studying what may eventually become your major. When you've given yourself some time to make sure that you've found the essential combination of interest and ability, then you can declare. Being an "Undeclared" isn't a bad thing. Having said all that, it's important to note that even if you do declare early, and then want to change your major, it's simply a matter of filling out a form. But leave your options open. You'll be better off in the long run.

The second common mistake is not thinking at all about your major. You might think of this at the "life happens" college strategy. While you don't have to pick your major now, you should shoot to have one set midway through your sophomore year. We both know people who took eighteen to twenty credits their second semester senior year. Sounds silly, right? Not if that's the only way you can graduate. Whether you try to or not, you cannot graduate without a major. This means that if you haven't declared, or even if you have declared, and going into your last semester you find yourself with only fifteen of the needed thirty-two credits in any particular department, you're going to be seriously bumming. As the rest of the graduating class is at the beach sick, you'll be struggling through five or six classes in your major (if your school will even let you take that many credits in one semester).

The moral of this story is not to take the shotgun blast approach to your course selection. We certainly advocate taking a sampling of many different course areas in school. In fact, at most "liberal arts" schools you'll be forced to do this. Nevertheless, remember that college has an ending point. If you want to reach it in a reasonable amount of time, you'll make sure you've picked a major by the middle of your sophomore year and have met the requirements at least one semester before graduation.

Things to Consider in Choosing Your Major

By this time you probably have gotten a sense of what to consider in choosing your major. Nonetheless, choosing a major seems to cause such stress among many students that we thought we'd get a little more specific on this issue.

Initially, you should consider that there are a number of things that go into doing well in a major (which should be every student's goal). You need to enjoy what you do in life and in school. We don't want to preach here, but it's very rare for people to be successful in something that they find personally unfulfilling. To echo a previous example, this means that if you're in love with the idea of being a doctor but you despise biology, chemistry, and physics, medicine's probably not for you.

In that same vein, it's important that you have some degree of aptitude in your chosen field. Different fields call for different skills, thought processes, and work habits. It is a fact of life that we are all born with different abilities. If you can't add ingredients, much less numbers, being a Geometry major is probably not for you. Conversely, if you don't have an artistic bone in your body, you're not going to enjoy being a Sculpting major. Being realistic in recognizing your strengths and weaknesses will help you find a major that's right for you.

Having said that, it's also important that you understand that choosing your major is not a life-changing decision. Simply because you've chosen a major does not mean that you are locked into a lifelong binding contract with a department. Everyone changes their major. There are people in school who have changed their major three or even four times. People sometimes do this for serious reasons, such as they're Political Science majors and fail "American Government." Sometimes they do it for selfish reasons, like they've found a psychology professor who doesn't believe in giving exams or grading lower than an A⁻. Moreover, sometimes students switch their major for no reason except to change. You can too.

There are always people in school who will tell you that they are such and such a major because that was the first department they found on campus, or that the professors are easy, or some other ridiculous reason. These people will then say that they don't really like their major, but they've taken three or four classes in it and don't want to feel like they've wasted their time. You know what? They've already wasted their time. Staying in a major you don't enjoy, aren't good at, or you don't think is adding to your education is foolish. Bag the major and find a new one.

Finally, you don't have to try and figure alone out what the right major is for you. In fact, there are a bunch of on-campus resources to help you make this decision. At some schools, you will, at first, be randomly assigned a faculty advisor. This professor may or may not have anything to do with your proposed topic of study. However, she will definitely have the experience of having helped students in the past, and having gone to college herself. In addition to making sure that you're taking classes and approving your schedule, your advisor should be able to help you sort out the different departments on campus, talk to other professors for you, and recommend courses for you.

> *"My advisor and mentor helped me to choose the major I felt most comfortable with and helped me to decide which classes I should take to achieve my degree."*
>
> *—Whittier College Student*

Most schools also now have a career placement center. Basically, a placement center is a clearinghouse for information on available jobs, job hunting strategies, and careers. The center should have information, for example, on what types of courses graduate schools and employers in particular fields look for from students graduating college. Moreover, they might be able to help you find careers in different fields that you didn't even know were out there. You should spend some time looking into what information your school has to offer regarding careers before choosing your major.

CHAPTER 4

You've Got Class

CLASS

At this point, it seems like they should award you a degree just for successfully making the transition to your new life at college—and maybe the Nobel Peace Prize for not killing your roommate. However, remember why you're really here: To party your tail off. Oops, who said that? Seriously now, you're here to get a college degree, and, not surprisingly, that entails going to class.

To Go, or Not To Go

"Going" is actually a key word. Before we say anything else, lets talk about attendance. One day, maybe a week or two into the semester, you wake up and realize that no one is keeping tabs on whether or not you go to class. Melanie had this epiphany around week three, when she realized that about twenty-five of the forty people in her 8 a.m. Bio class showed up on a regular basis. Everyone showed up to hand in papers, etcetera, but not many were into the early morning rally. This freedom can be a great thing. If you have a big exam in the afternoon, you may decide to cut your morning class to study. Or, you may wake up on a Friday morning and swear that you'll never drink tequila again, if you can just go back to sleep for another two hours.

The sky is not going to fall if you miss a couple of classes, but keep a couple of things in mind. Most professors do care if you come to class. As we discussed earlier, they're not like high school teachers who are going to call your parents or give you a detention for cutting class. But they're also going to remember your empty seat when they're giving out grades. Think of attendance as an insurance policy. If you choke on a test or have to hand in a paper a day late, your professor is a lot more likely to cut you a break if she knows that you've been in class. Regular attendance is also going to make studying for exams much easier. Ever try to teach yourself three months worth of material in a night? Unfortunately, at some point you probably will, and it isn't easy. Even if you only missed a few classes, and you get filled in by a friend, you'll find you never get as much out of someone else's notes as you do from your own. And one more thing. We told you before that what professors actually teach in class may or may not be anything like what was on the syllabus. This means that you may read everything that's on the schedule and find that it only prepares you for one of the exam's four questions. So take it easy with the cuts. You're not doing yourself any favors by skipping class.

The Syllabus: What It Is and How To Use It

Now that we've decided that you're going to class (right?), let talk about the backbone of most courses, the syllabus. The first session of almost every class consists of the professor handing out this multi-page document and telling you a bit about what you can expect for the semester. You may have had a syllabus for a high school class, but probably nothing this detailed. On it are what you need to read for each class, due dates for papers and projects, and the dates of your exams. These game plans can be really useful for managing your schedule. Sit down with a date/assignment book and the syllabi (cool plural) for all of your courses, and write down the dates of your papers and exams. This way you'll notice if you have three papers due in one week, or a French quiz and your English exam on the same day. Don't worry, as long as you note these tight spots in advance, you can make sure you give yourself enough time to prepare for them.

Let us tell you now that while paper and test dates rarely change, professors don't always stay on top of the reading schedules. Certain topics and books—usually the professor's favorites—inevitably take up more class time than they were originally allotted. Professors deal with this in different ways. They may squish the last three weeks of material into two classes (always a fun approach) or cut some parts out of the syllabus. What we're saying is don't waste your time writing all of your reading assignments into your calendar. One of Melanie's compulsively organized friends spent hours writing her reading assignments for each class into her date book, each in a different colored ink. Nice idea, but she ended up with a beautiful but completely useless bunch of reminders.

Use your syllabus wisely. Note where you are after each class, so you know what to expect in the next session. The professor probably won't remind you after Tuesday's class what to read before you meet on Thursday. That doesn't mean she won't ask you a question at that next class and expect you to know what she's talking about. Keeping up with the reading can be particularly important in certain class formats. In fact, now is a good time to talk a little about the different kinds of classes you can take.

Know What You're Getting Yourself Into

When you register for classes, you're not only picking the subjects of your courses, you're picking their format. Most often you'll choose between two main types of classes: lectures and seminars. You'll do just fine in either format, but it will help if you know what to expect.

Lecture courses are usually open to a greater number of students, which means the class size is bigger. If you've heard the term "lecture hall," this is where it comes from. These classes are held in big rooms, often with desks on several tiers, with a podium at the front for the professor. As a freshman, you take a lot of intro-level lecture classes. These will probably be big, because so many students need to take them. If you go to a large school, they can be really big— bring your binoculars. Lecture courses can have so many students that interaction is not a key element here. The professor lectures, and you take notes. Period. He or she will probably ask questions or ask for comments, but responding is often voluntary on your part.

Seminars, on the other hand, are small classes, usually no more than twenty students. Here you may sit with your desks in a circle, or sit around one large table. The size and set-up are this way because in seminars interaction is the key. Instead of giving a lecture, the professor guides a discussion of the topic. You're supposed to learn from other students' perceptions, as well as from your professor's ideas and opinions. As you may have guessed, staying on top of your assignments is essential in a seminar, because you will be expected to contribute to the discussion in every class.

Right now you may be thinking, "All right, I'll take lecture classes so I don't have to talk, and I can get away without doing the reading." Not so fast. We said you probably wouldn't be forced to talk in a lecture class. We didn't say the professor wouldn't notice if you never opened your mouth. Most professors remember who participated in class when they're giving out the grades. Or, conversely, it's not a good thing if a professor can't remember you at all. The impersonal atmosphere of a big class can be great on the days when you want to blend in with the walls, but it can be a drawback if you want some personal attention. It's harder to get help from a professor when there are 100 other students in the class. Lectures are also the place where you run into teaching assistants, who, as we discussed earlier, can be either a blessing or a curse. Basically, lectures are a nice, relatively unintimidating way to get your feet wet in college classes, but don't take advantage of the format to slack off. Sliding through the semester, doing as little work as possible will not help you when exams roll around.

Seminars may sound a little intense to you, probably because this format isn't used too often in high school. This format is usually used for more advanced courses. However, some schools specifically design seminars for freshman, to prepare you for what's ahead. You don't want to sign up for an advanced Shakespeare seminar your first semester, unless you feel ready to contribute to discussions of irony in Elizabethan literature. Our friend Bill decided to take an advanced French seminar his freshman year, not realizing that the entire class and all discussion was to be, in fact, in French. He survived, but he did look at the course descriptions more closely afterwards. But you could take a Psychology seminar on group dynamics, where the only requirement is being willing to work with the group. You will have to take a seminar at some point, to fulfill the upper-level requirements of your major, so you might as well dive in and get used to this format.

Speak Up!

You noticed that much of the descriptions of class format revolve around speaking in class. There's no way to get around it, taking part in class discussions is very important in college. In a high school each class had some combo of quizzes, tests, group projects, papers, and maybe even an oral report that contributed to your grade. If you didn't say much in class, at least there was some other way for the teacher to know if you had any clue about what was going on. In college, you may only get two grades for an entire class— a midterm and a paper, a midterm and a final, etcetera. If you don't speak up, you're not giving your professor anything else to go on when she determines your grade. Some professors will let you know that participation is a required part of class, and some won't. We recommend that you take part no matter what. Why? Imagine this: you got an D on your midterm and a B on your final. If your professor remembers that you always made an effort to contribute to class discussions, we're betting that your final grade is a lot closer to the B. Afraid of making a stupid comment? It may sound harsh, but it's better to speak up and find out that you're on the wrong track than to find out when you get your paper back that you didn't understand what was going on.

If you're terrified of getting called on, take proactive measures. Think of a couple of questions or comments when you do your reading. Raise your hand, take a deep breath, and ask a question. There, you participated without being put on the spot to answer a question. Professors like to know that you're interested and doing your work, and they usually don't care if it's you or them that initiates your comment. Of course we've never done this (yeah, right), but we've heard that this is also a good tactic if you haven't done all of your reading for class. If you make a comment on the part of the reading that you did do, the professor will probably leave you alone for the rest of the class.

We do recommend that you speak up in class. However, you're not in a competition with the professor to get the most air time. To reiterate what we said above in the section about professors, no one, especially the professor, likes a student who comments on everything. We guarantee that you will run into one of these creatures at some point in your college career, and we sincerely hope that it's not you. The class blabbermouth usually likes to argue every point in the sincere belief that her opinion is extremely valuable, and she usually interrupts frequently with her oh-so-interesting comments and anecdotes. Sound annoying? If you think you're annoyed, imagine how the professor feels. This kind of contribution to class will hurt you, not help you.

We should also mention that there may be some classes, lecture or not, where contributing will not be a matter of choice. Some professors make a seating chart, call on each student, and write down your ability to respond next to your name. This can be intimidating, but there's only one solution: Make sure you do the reading.

Taking Notes

Good notes are an important part of good grades. You can come up with some pretty cool doodles in a two-hour lecture period (like Joe's T.A. lecture class), but most professors don't give credit for these on exams. There's no one correct way to take notes. Everyone develops a personalized system. Until you discover exactly what works for you, here are a few general suggestions:

- You don't have to write down every word a professor says. You couldn't do this even if you wanted to. If you don't believe us, try to copy the dialogue from a "Seinfeld" episode for a few minutes. You probably won't even be able to catch half of what Kramer says!

- Take down a basic outline of the lecture. Most professors give their lectures from an outline, so it shouldn't be too hard to write down what they're saying in outline form. This doesn't mean Roman numerals and lettered subheads. Start the main points at the margin and move in toward the middle of the paper with supporting points. As a law student, Joe's turned this into an art. No one else knows what the hell his notes say because of weird signals telling you to look other places and dots emphasizing or de-emphasizing some point. He likes it that way. Find your own outlining techniques and you will too.

- Abbreviate. Just make sure you use abbreviations you can decipher later. For example don't write down "ex." You'll never know whether you meant "explain," "example," "extra," or something else.

- Put the date at the top of each day's notes, so you can look back later at particular classes. Make sure you also put where your notes for a particular day stop.

Otherwise you'll think you missed some important and relevant issue transition.

- Keep up with your reading, so you understand what the heck the professor is talking about.
- If your professor writes something on the board, it's a good indication that you should have it in your notes. Of course, Melanie had a professor who occasionally wrote a couple words of complete gibberish on the board just to see how many students were diligently copying them into their notes.
- This sounds obvious, but write neatly. Your notes are useless if you can't decipher them a month later. Find a pen that really works for you. Melanie always took her notes with a purple, Pilot, fine point pen. Joe still makes fun of her for this, but her notes always looked beautiful. If you have lousy handwriting, consider taking your notes on a laptop.

You'll find that class notes vary in importance from class to class. If your professor is basically reiterating the reading in her lectures, you don't have to take as many notes. On the other hand, if your professor is expanding on what is covered in the reading (or talking about things that are nowhere to be found in the reading), your notes become much more valuable. It'll take a couple of classes to figure this out, so we advise you stick with note-taking until the class is really off the ground. By then you'll know what the deal is and you can adapt your studying and note-taking techniques to fit the course.

Reading

Whether it's in the process of studying for an exam, or just keeping up with daily assignments, you have to do a lot of reading in college— probably much more than you did in high school. The number one problem freshmen have with reading is that they don't do it. We're telling you right now: Keep up with your reading. On September 20, it may seem like you have plenty of time to catch up before exams, but by December 5, you're going to have a backlog of thousands of pages, and you're not going to get it done. If you do fall behind in your reading, start to get back on track by doing the reading for the classes you have coming up. If you try to start back where you stopped not only won't you catch up, but you won't be able to participate in or fully understand what's going on in class now. If you get behind in a class, keep up with your daily assignments, and gradually catch up on the rest by tacking on a little each day. If you try to read a whole novel in a day, you won't remember any of it even if you do get through it.

Many freshman panic because they think they can't read fast enough to get it all done. If you feel this way, take a step back and think about how you're attacking your reading. We bet that the reason it's taking so long is that you're trying too hard to absorb every teensy weensy little bit of what you're reading. Don't try to memorize as you read. Unless you have a photographic memory it's not going to work. You have to read at a pace fast enough to keep yourself interested. If you slow down and agonize over each sentence not only will your thoughts start to drift, but you'll be so caught up in the pieces that you won't see the big picture.

Try reading through each assignment at a steady, fairly quick, pace. Use a highlighter to mark passages that contain important facts or ideas. When you're done you can go back over your highlights to remember the main points and form an overall opinion. Your highlights will also help you review for exams. We should warn you right now that it will take you a few weeks to get the knack for highlighting what's important. Not that either of us ever did this, but at first you may find you're highlighting more than you're leaving white, because everything sounds important. One of the reasons you need to keep up with your reading assignments is that you can take your book to class and compare what you've highlighted to what the professor points out as important. Soon you'll be highlighting like a pro. By the end of your four years, you'll barely be able to read the Sunday paper without feeling the need to mark important passages.

PROFESSORS

These Ain't High School Teachers

Almost everyone who's gone to high school was told at one time or another that once they got to college there wouldn't be anyone to hold their hand, tell them to do their homework, or force them to study for their exams. In large part, this is true. Professors are far different in college from teachers in high school.

It's likely that you knew some fine teachers in high school, and some teachers you're happy to get away from. Either way you're likely to immediately recognize a change when you start classes your freshman year. In all fairness to high school teachers, they have to work with students who are varied in intellectual ability, work habits, and interest. Moreover, they are told what to teach by the school system in the state and are discouraged from importing bias, opinion, and occasionally, creativeness into the class room. College professors are free from these restraints for several reasons.

First, whereas you had to go to high school, you want to go to college. This means that college professors expect you to come to class, pay attention, and do the work they suggest. Yeah, that's right, "suggest." The majority of professors care about their jobs and want to educate their students. However, professors will tell you that students who don't come to class and do the course work make grading easier because it's simple to fail them. You won't get a meeting with your guidance counselor, or a warning notice in your mailbox. In fact it's likely that your professors won't take attendance or even ask to see the homework. Instead, they'll be able to see immediately based on your exam who really knows what's going on in the course.

One other hint here: Because professors assume that you are in college to learn, they only are interested in assisting those students who are doing the work. Quite frankly, professors don't have the time or the incentive to answer questions in their office that were answered at a class you cut. The flip side of this coin is that professors are generally very receptive to students who are making a sincere effort and are still struggling with the course.

Second, college professors are interested in the courses they teach. In fact, in many cases, professors have devoted their entire lives to the study of a specific subject. This concept, so totally different from high school, plays out in many ways. For example, your Physics professor may have a law of physics named after her, your English professor may have won the Nobel prize for literature, your Government professor may be a former member of the United States Senate, and your Journalism professor may have to cut class short on Wednesdays so he can do the five o'clock news. In short, professors care about their courses because it's often their life's passion. As a result, they are not going to be timid; they are going to be opinionated. They're likely to bait you and trap you in arguments to teach you how to debate. They don't feel like they have to follow a script or a course plan. Heck, they're going to write the exam anyway; if you cover one thing instead of the other, they'll just leave that out of the test. Professors will even import their experience into the class to get you excited about the subject. How many people had high school teachers like that?

Moreover, professors can vary the courses they teach from semester to semester, so they don't get bored from repetition. If they taught "Feminist Literature" last semester, just to spice it up they might teach "Men in American Novels" this semester. As a result, not only do the students get a variety of courses to take, professors stay interested.

Third, teaching is usually only one part of a college professor's life. Many professors are actually practicing what they teach. Teaching offers professors a way to make money to live while providing them with the resources and time they need to do what really turns them on. Professors may be interested in doing research in a particular field and need the library, the biology center, the multimedia center, or whatever. The point here is that college professors aren't living for you. Several things happen as a result.

One is that professors aren't always going to be around. If you have a question, need to discuss paper topics, or want to go over an exam, you're going to have to fit their office hours into your schedule, or make an appointment to see them. Professors may have different reactions to this, but our experience is that if you just show up at their office, they're likely to politely tell you to make an appointment because they're busy (and they're telling the truth).

Another consequence of professors not only being teachers is that they make you their pet projects for the semester. In other words, whatever they are currently interested in may become what you learn, rather than what you thought you signed up for. This is especially true in introductory survey courses designed to provide general education on a subject. It's not unheard of for an introductory business course to turn into a seminar on Pacific Rim economics. This is great if you're psyched to learn about Japanese trade strategy, but a bummer if you thought you were going to learn the laws of supply and demand.

Fourth, college professors are secure in their knowledge and their profession. We think that this security translates into respect for their students. We've found that professors are interested in talking to their students, listening to their comments and constructively aiding in their education. College professors are willing to let the class delve into difficult and confrontational topics. For that matter, professors will let a class struggle with a question that may not have an answer. They do this because they know they can control the flow of the discussion, and are intrigued instead of intimidated by the prospect of hearing new perspectives on different issues. In short, college professors automatically convey respect to their students and treat them as adults. Their respect is yours to lose.

Fifth, there seems to be a strong barrier between students and teachers at the high school level. The same is not true in college. Hand in hand with professors treating students like adults is the idea that college professors may be more social and develop friendships with students. College campuses are, in many respects, little worlds unto their own. This is true at colleges of all sizes. As a result, a real feeling of community develops. Professors, as well as Deans and other administrators, will attend many functions that are student-based or organized, and selected students may be invited to many university functions. Who gets invited depends on what students are involved in. Nonetheless, these gatherings provide opportunities for members of the academic community to interact, and unlike in high school, for all the groups to mix. It wouldn't be unusual to have a Dean and her husband, a professor and his wife, and a group of students seated at the same dinner table.

Less formal settings may also present themselves. Jeez, that sounded stuffy. Put differently, you may hang with your professors. We've both been invited to professors' homes for small dinner parties and large informal gatherings. It's a very cool thing to get a letter from a professor inviting you and some students to a barbecue at his home. You find out that your professors are real people with families, pets, and bad art. The same English professor who teaches you Shakespeare may really dig Eric Clapton. For that matter, she may pick up a guitar and play Eric Clapton. "Layla . . . You've got me on my knees . . . Layla . . . I'm beggin', darlin', please . . . " You get the idea.

"Professors are everywhere, not just in the classroom. They're in the audience at athletic events and theater performances, on the court in intramural basketball games, and in the dining halls just hanging out."

—*Wheaton College Student*

"Professors allow you to call them at home, and sometimes they invite you over."

—*Wittenberg University Student*

"The professors are great. They are very personable and willing to help. They often support us by attending concerts, athletic tournaments, or plays."

—*Wittenberg University Student*

Developing friendships with your professors is a tremendous opportunity. They will have done interesting things in their lives to get where they are now, which may be useful to you just beginning your education. Moreover, you will need recommendations somewhere down the line. Unquestionably, the professor who knows you and your background will write you a better recommendation than the one who only knows your grade. Finally, the professors that want to interact with their students are good people. They have deliberately chosen to make an effort to get to know their students. Take advantage of this. You'll be happy you did.

One last caveat, not all professors will meet any or all of the descriptions we've laid out above. It would be impossible for us to try and map out every potential character trait you might encounter. The main point is that your relationship with your professors in college will be distinct from that which you had with your high school teachers. Anticipate and enjoy the change.

Teaching Assistants

In high school, most people had one teacher for every class. An upperclassman was probably never called into your freshman English class to explain and discuss your assignments with you. Well, welcome to another collegiate change.

In college most professors have teaching assistants. T.A.s, as they are commonly referred to, are usually graduate students in the department in which your professor teaches. Their function is simple: They help the professor teach the class. Professors may have many T.A.s and may use them in different ways. Before we discuss how T.A.s function though, you need to know why they're here in the first place.

There are a couple of reasons why a professor may have a T.A. For example, the T.A.s department requires that its graduate students teach at least one semester. This is probably the least favorable scenario for you because the T.A. might not be very good at teaching, even if he or she wants to be. Joe had one T.A. in school who was petrified of teaching and looked like she hadn't been out of the library since the late 1960s. She basically read the course book to the class for four months. Joe's still waiting for the Guggenheim Museum to contact him about his doodling collection from that class. It's a real bummer when you have a T.A. who's just filling his requirements and comes to class and reads a prepared text at you, but it happens.

Another reason you can find yourself with a T.A. is that the professor teaching the course feels that, for some reason, such as the size of the class, she needs a T.A., and has chosen this one because of her interest in and aptitude for the subject. This can be great for you. If the professor is basically unreachable and has a line around the block for his one hour of office hours, your T.A. may be able to field some questions. For that matter, we have a friend who told us that she had a class with a foreign professor whose accent was so thick that he couldn't understand a word of what the man was saying. The T.A. basically retaught the class in English so that the students could learn the material. On the other hand, if the T.A. only took the job because she felt obligated to the professor to do so, or some other similar reason, the same problems discussed above can occur.

"Several of my professors don't even speak clear English, and therefore it's extremely hard to understand them."

—James Madison University Student

"I don't like the idea so much of the use of T.A.'s teaching classes. I pay tuition to get taught by professors—not other students."

—University of California at Davis Student

You might end up with a T.A. because the T.A.s singular goal in life is to teach your professor's subject and he's pleaded with the professor to be given the chance. This is probably the best scenario for you, because although the T.A. may be a little bit obsessed, he'll want to be there. He'll also be trying to impress the professor to get his approval and recommendation for a teaching position. If the class is bored to death and not learning anything, the T.A. isn't going to get his recommendation. As a result, the T.A. will likely enjoy class discussions, be energetic, and want to help you learn. Bonus for you.

Regardless of how they attained their T.A. status, all T.A.s generally function the same way. When the Professor lectures during your class time, the T.A. will be there taking notes like the rest of you. Then, the professor will probably have the T.A. schedule a weekly time for the class to meet without him. If the class is large, there may be more than one T.A. and the class will be divided into sections with each one assigned a particular T.A. During the weekly meeting time your T.A. will probably give your class or section a mini-lecture on some topic related to your professor's lecture. Then for the rest of the allotted time, you'll discuss the topic and you'll have the opportunity to ask any questions you need to ask. This can be really helpful, especially when you're struggling with a difficult subject and the professor keeps explaining it the same confusing way over and over again. Having a T.A. explain something in a slightly different way might help make it click for you. T.A.s will also have office hours at different times from your professor's. If you can't get in to see your professor, or, for example, you're too embarrassed to ask your professor what you think is a simple question, you can approach your T.A. during his or her office hours.

The other thing T.A.s are great for is review sessions. At the end of the semester when you're freaking out and have studied so much that everything is beginning to blur, a T.A.s review session can really put you on the right track. By the time of the review session, the T.A. has probably seen the exam and will subtly help you feel out the important points in the course. Or not so subtly. One of us (we won't say who) had a T.A. slip and announce one of the three essay questions on the final exam. Let's just say that it's a lot easier to do well on an exam when you start with 33 percent of a perfect score.

However, don't substitute the T.A.s explanation for something the professor explained differently, even if it seems correct. In other words, on an exam, always explain a concept the professor's way, never the T.A.s way. The obvious exception to this is if in one of your review sessions the T.A. announces "the professor missed something the other day" or "Professor Smith asked me to expand on . . ." Otherwise, always go with the professor's explanation.

My Professor Hates Me

Maybe. Yes, we know you expected to hear some reassurance that professors don't ever hate students or that it could be that your professor is having a bad day. Unfortunately, that's not always the case. As in real life, in college people don't always get along. The truth is that it happened in high school too, except that your teachers felt like they had to mask it. In college, professors have a greater degree of autonomy and rarely feel as if they should shield you from their thoughts.

At the outset, it really is unlikely that your professor hates you. This probably isn't what you want to hear, but it's our experience that most professors don't care enough about their students to waste the emotional energy involved in hating you. There are certain professors that you'll develop professional and friendly relationships with, but the majority of the time there is a simple, almost detached, relationship between professors and students. As a result, there isn't really the opportunity for your professor to hate you. A professor might think you're irritating, annoying, arrogant, dull, or maybe even a little dense, but they probably don't hate you.

So how can you avoid any animosity between you and your professor? The answer is basically common sense. You simply need to avoid calling negative attention to yourself. In college people draw negative attention to themselves in different ways, but there are a few that professors find universally annoying. For example, professors don't like people who don't do the work in their class, and it's usually obvious to everyone who these people are. When your assignment was to read Shakespeare and you explain to the class that Hamlet drove his Jeep to pick up Ophelia on their date, the professor's not going to be happy.

Another good way to escape drawing negative attention to yourself is to avoid excessive talking in class. No one, including professors, likes someone who's only contributing in class because they like to hear the sound of their own voice. Don't take this the wrong way. Interacting with your professor is a necessary part of your education and essential if you want to get a good grade. When you have something to say that substantively adds to the class, you should absolutely participate. However, if someone else had already made your point, or if you can tell the professor is trying to bring the discussion to a close, wait until you have an appropriate opportunity to make your comment. By the way, just in case you slip and screw up by making an ill-timed or silly comment, you should know that it happens all the time. What we're talking about here is a pattern of excessive in-class speech.

There's one last way people draw negative attention to themselves. We'll call them "stargazers." There are always one or two people in every class who constantly approach the professor right after the class ends and are always there for his office hours. We even know of people who have called their professor a couple of times at home. The fact is that, as we've said before, professors are generally interested in helping their students learn the material. If you have a legitimate need to speak to your professor you should approach him. For example, approaching him after class for a minute may save his time during office hours. Furthermore, if the professor has given you his home number and you have a time-sensitive question, give him a call. Having said that, don't become a "stargazer." These people are like stalkers and they annoy professors. No professor wants to dread running into a student in the cafeteria or the walkway because they know they are going to be deluged by questions about class. The last thing you want is to have your professor avoiding you because he finds you irritating. Professors are people too. When you need them, go talk to them. When you don't need them, leave them alone. When you run into them outside the classroom, realize that not every comment you make has to be about the subject they teach. Professors may like you more if you talk to them about the football scores or the car you drive!

Well, now that we've talked about how to avoid animosity between you and your professor, we need to discuss what to do if, despite your best efforts, you don't get along. We suppose the first point is that you should probably suck it up and try and pull through. We've never heard of a professor who has used their personal feelings to grade a student in their class. This means that although you might despise class, which a professor can make miserable for an individual, as long as you do the work and study, your grade in the class will probably be unaffected.

There are a couple of other things you can do. For example, find out if you still have time to drop the class and add the same class with a different professor or a new class entirely. Classes that you need in order to fill a requirement or as a prerequisite to some other class are generally taught by more than one professor and several times a year. If you can't deal with your Anthropology professor, chances are you'll have the opportunity to take it with a different professor.

Another course of action is to go and talk to your professor about the problem. We're not sure how we feel about this, but we felt obligated to mention it. It's our opinion that this is a chancy proposition. On the one hand, you may go talk to your professor and she may laugh it off and reassure you that nothing is wrong. That would be great. However, on the other hand, you may go to your professor and he may tell you that he finds you cocky, or ill-prepared, or something similarly offensive. Worse yet, he may tell you straight-facedly that there's no problem but become offended or, at least, aware, that you think there is a problem. Now you've drawn negative attention to yourself. No professor likes to be told that a student suspects him of negative bias. That's also a serious charge to make against a professor. If you choose this route, tread extremely lightly.

Time for a little story about professors hating students. When Joe was in college, as part of his major he had to take a class called

"Democracy and Dictatorship." He thought the class should be called "Communism" because the professor spent every class extolling the virtues of Marx and providing pointed examples of how the capitalist economy in the U.S. was a failure. Joe quickly adopted a defensive position and began to regularly point out that if the professor hated our system of government so much, a simple solution for us all would be for him to leave. Anyway, Joe and Professor Marx didn't get along so well. Joe was scared because the only assignment in the class was to keep a journal based on your personal reaction to the assigned readings. Great situation, right? The professor doesn't like Joe in class, now he's going to read a collection of Joe's writings and give him a grade. When Joe got his grade back, it was just okay. He was positive that it had to do with the professor's personal feelings rather than his journal. So, Joe made an appointment to go see the professor. He got himself all worked up to get into a drop-down, drag-out argument. When Joe walked into his professor's office, though, the man was all smiles. He asked if he could ask Joe a favor: Would he be willing to read his latest manuscript and comment on it before it was published? What? Joe thought this guy hated him, but now he's saying that because he respected his input he'd like his comments on his latest work. It caught Joe so off-guard that he simply took the manuscript and left the office, forgetting to discuss the journal. However, it did get Joe thinking. Perhaps his writings were a little biased. Maybe it was true that he had gotten frustrated with the readings for the class. Maybe Professor Marx really wasn't concerned with what Joe wrote, but instead, with how he wrote it.

Well, Joe still gets angry about that grade because he knows he's flawless. Nonetheless, the point here is simple. Don't give up on professors or their class because you don't get along. Not everyone in life gets along. Moreover, sometimes things aren't always as they appear. Just be yourself and work hard. No dislike between you and your professor can take away your effort and subsequent understanding of the subject. Remember, you're really there to get an education— not be your professor's best buddy.

CHAPTER 5

When The Pressure Is On

STUDYING

You need to study in college. You can't get away with a half-hearted effort. We probably wouldn't explain this concept in this way to the whole world, but we know that our readers are at a higher level of comprehension than many high school students. In high school, putting in a little bit of time, work, and energy puts you ahead of many of your classmates because they're doing *nothing*. Let's face it, we all knew a bunch of people in high school who were more concerned with playing Nintendo or listening to the Grateful Dead than anything going on in school. As a result, they helped elevate your grades by their poor performance. What we're getting at here is that you were bound to look good when surrounded by a bunch of clowns. This is not going to happen in college.

In college you'll find that everyone has gotten there because they were ahead of the pack in high school. Moreover, college students have a greater incentive to study because they're paying for their education, and they're devoting an additional four years of their lives to the effort of getting a degree. Simply put, the level of competition has gone up since high school. If you decide to go to graduate school, the level of competition will go up again for the same reason. Nonetheless, in college you will not be surrounded by a bunch of unconcerned students. Everyone will be concerned about his or her performance. This means that the same level of effort that put you above the average in high school will put you below the average in college.

Many Roads to Success: Different Study Techniques

Now that we've agreed you'll need to study, you'll need to know how. Successful study techniques vary from person to person. Melanie likes to recopy her notes a few times, each time condensing them more, so what starts out as thirty pages of detailed notes ends up as a seven page outline of the most important concepts. As she cuts down what's written on the pages, she increases the amount she can fill in from memory. Something about writing helps her remember things. Joe, on the other hand, finds that re-reading his notes several times is more helpful than rewriting them. You'll gradually find what works best for you too. Here are some tips to get you started:

- Adapt your study techniques to fit the material on which you're being tested. If you're preparing for an exam, Bio 101 for example, for which you need to know a lot of definitions, you may find **flash cards** helpful. For a math-based class like Physics or Calculus, **practice problems** are essential to your study plans. For a Political Science or History exam, it may be more important that you **outline** the material, so events are tied together in your mind. Similarly, you can memorize facts for a multiple-choice exam, but for an essay exam you need to come prepared with opinions and facts to support them.

- Study along the way. This sounds obvious, but it can save you from night—before—the—exam panic attacks. Especially in courses such as Chemistry, where you are required to do a lot of rote memorization, you should work incrementally. Try to memorize as much as possible each week. You'll still have to go back and review before the exam, but that's a lot easier than trying to cram a million definitions and formulas into your brain at the last minute.

- Look at past exams. Most professors make their old exams available to students, usually putting them on reserve at the library. What better way to gauge what will be on your exam than to see what the professor has asked in the past. Your ability to answer the questions on the old tests also tells you if you know the material.

- Look through your notes for clues on what will be on the exam. Even if you can't look at past exams, you can often figure out what's going to be on the test by looking at your notes. Look for themes that your professor has addressed in relation to each topic covered. For example, if your English professor talked about the use of nature imagery five times during the semester, there's a good chance that there will be a question about this on the exam. If your Political Science prof kept asking how the Cold War influenced policy and decision-making, get ready to answer a question about its impact.

- Ask upperclassmen to tell you about past exams. In case you haven't figured it out yet, we're recommending that you get as good an idea as possible of what's going to be on the test. It may not be a good idea to take one person's word for it, but if several people tell you that a professor's exams always center on the reading for the course, not on the class notes (or vice versa), it can really help you direct your study efforts.

- Join a study group. Getting together with other students in your class can be a big help. It usually turns out that each person has a different point of expertise, so you can ask each other questions and clarify things for one another. By listening to how other people would answer a question, you can see where you might have missed something. You can also help each other fill in any gaps in your notes. Just make sure you join a group with people who have done their homework; spending an hour filling someone else in on the basics won't be much help. Likewise, make sure you know your stuff before you get together with the group.

- Use mnemonics and acronyms to help you with memorization. For example, if you have to memorize the elements of DNA, guanine, cytosine, adenine, and thiamine, you could use the mnemonic Gabe Crawled Around Texas or the acronym GCAT.

- DON'T PANIC. No matter how bad the situation is, freaking out is going to make it worse.

"Students here revere academics and nothing else. That's the way it should be. Get drunk, get naked, but only after you study your butt off."

—**Rice University Student**

Get Help

If you need some extra help in certain subjects, there are several ways you can supplement your own study efforts. One of the best methods is to get a tutor. A good way to start your search for a tutor is to ask your professor. Most academic departments keep a list of the students they recommend as tutors, and not only will your professor be able to give you this list, but by asking for it you let your professor know that you care enough about the class to look for extra help. Don't make the mistake of letting your tutor do your thinking for you. Put hard work into each assignment, and *then* let your tutor go over your work with you to point out the areas where you need improvement. Since tutors have usually had classes with your professors, they're also good sources of advice on what specific profs look for in class and on exams.

Professors themselves are a good source of help, although they can't usually give you as much time as a tutor can. If you're struggling to come up with a paper topic or are worried that you don't understand a concept discussed in class, make an appointment to talk about your concerns. Just make sure that you think out what you want to ask ahead of time, and go in prepared to have a discussion. As we told you in chapter 4, professors aren't interested in doing your work for you. Later in the semester, when a professor has seen some of your work, on an early paper or exam, he or she can give good suggestions for improvement.

Lab work is another good way to reinforce what you've learned in class and get some extra practice before the exam. You may think that only science classes have labs—not true! Most schools also offer language labs, where you can go listen to tapes and practice your speaking. And libraries often offer audio-visual equipment that you can use to listen to tapes or watch videos as supplements to many of your classes.

Another useful study aid is one that you've probably heard of before: Cliffs Notes. Actually there are many different brands of commercial study outlines that cover subjects from literature to calculus. Before you get too excited, the way you *should* use these outlines may not be something you've heard before. These are not substitutes for doing assigned reading; they're supplements to help you with your assignments. For instance, if your English professor is pointing out imagery in *King Lear* that makes you think you read the wrong play, it may help you to buy an outline for the next play you read. After you read each scene, look at what the outline points out as important themes, images, symbols, etcetera. This will help you learn what to look for. An outline for a Chemistry class will help in a different way. It will summarize what textbooks take longer to say, and give you a basic outline to study from. Think you can get away with only reading an outline? Good luck. A couple years of teaching is all it takes for a professor to learn exactly what Cliffs has to say, and she won't appreciate finding it in your exam.

A Note About Procrastination

One of Melanie's roommates in college started her freshman year as a *serious* procrastinator. She would talk a lot about how she needed to start studying, but typically wouldn't take action until 10:00 the night before her 8 a.m. exam. Luckily she's a smart girl, so at first she escaped any serious consequences from her study habits. Well, second semester she had a tough course on International Politics, and although she worked hard in class, she put off studying for the cumulative exam until late the night before. When panic set in, she bought a six-pack of Coke and kept herself up all night cramming. By the time she arrived at the exam she knew her stuff. She sat down, started on the first essay question, and promptly drifted off to sleep—at least her brain did. Apparently her hand kept writing as her fatigued brain confusedly blended the facts with her dreams. As a result, her answer read something like this: "Linda and I went to the Russian church where the nuclear weapons are stored, but the bus was late and the CIA arrested us for underage drinking and roommate problems." The professor certainly got a kick out of grading this exam, but that didn't convince him to give her a decent grade.

Not many students are capable of writing an essay answer in their sleep, but many do lower their grades by procrastinating their way out of the time they need to study. This is not to say that procrastination isn't totally normal. Most people need to feel a little pressure to get motivated. And it's totally understandable that you'd much rather be hanging out with your friends, working out in the gym, going to a concert, or writing an article for the paper than studying for an exam. However, if you've convinced yourself that you'd really rather scrub the floor of your room with a toothbrush, or that you should volunteer to re-catalog the books in the library before you crack open the books, you've gone beyond acceptable dawdling and into the realm of serious procrastination.

You may find yourself procrastinating because you think you know a subject pretty well, and you don't think you need much time to study. Believe us, you won't feel that way once you sit down and start looking back over a semester's worth of material. On the other hand, you may feel overwhelmed by the amount of material you have to cover and procrastinate because you don't know where to start. In this case, you have to force yourself to dive in. We're betting that after a few hours of studying, you'll start to feel less intimidated. And, worst case scenario, if you slacked off all semester and there really *is* too much for you to learn in time for the exam, you have to study at least enough to pass the class.

Here are a few tips for conquering procrastination:

- Figure out where you are most likely to procrastinate, and study somewhere else. Thus if you talk on the phone or reorganize your sock drawer when you try to study in your room, you should go to the library. And if you're tempted to socialize with your friends in the library, you should stay in your room.

- Build a safe amount of procrastination time into your schedule. If you start studying at 11 a.m. on Sunday morning, plan to turn the football game on for an hour at 2:00 or go hang out in a friend's room for an hour at 3:00.

- Think about how much time you think you need to study for a class, and allot yourself twice that amount of time. You can always stop studying when you know the material, but there's no buying time if you start too late.

- Make a pact with a friend to keep each other in line. Sometimes you need a little willpower from someone else.

Cramming and the All-nighter

As you may have noticed, most of our suggestions for studying and getting extra help have something in common: They require time. Building a comprehensive understanding of a subject is not *supposed* to happen overnight. Nevertheless, we are not naive. We know that sometimes one night is all you have. For whatever reason, you have arrived at the night before your exam and you have no clue. Yes, you are about to participate in the time-dishonored tradition of The All-nighter.

Don't panic. It's way too late for that. What we're talking now is damage control, so stop crying because you're not going to get an "A," and start doing what needs to be done to get you the best possible grade under the circumstances. We also recommend that you do get at least a little sleep. (Remember the earlier story of Melanie's friend who didn't.) If you have to get up at 8:00, try to get in bed by 3:00, so you can rest your eyes and let your brain untangle a little before the exam.

Start by taking a look at how much material you have to cover and making yourself a schedule. If it's 8 p.m., you have seven hours to study before your 3 a.m. deadline. You need to be halfway through the material by 11:30. This sounds simple, but the temptation will be to spend as long on each topic as you would if you had plenty of time to study. If you're going to do the caffeine thing, don't go crazy. Too much caffeine will turn you into a useless spaz who's more likely to break something than memorize anything. Stay far away from No Doz and similar over-the-counter stimulants, which can make you so wired that you can't focus on anything. We'll talk about drugs later, but people who use such substances can get hooked on things like cocaine in a situation like this. You won't have to worry about your exam if you're dead. You get the point.

EXAMS

Why Exams ?

Professors give exams to deprive college students of sleep and fun time. Okay, maybe that's not really the reason. It could be that professors give exams because they're required to by the school or because they actually care whether or not you are taking in and understanding the information being taught in the course. We realize that the reasons behind the need for exams seem straightforward at first glance. However, if you take just a couple of minutes to think about the practical application of exams in college today, we think you'll be better prepared to take one.

Throughout the book we've tried to remind you that although college is an adventure and not solely focused on your classroom studies, you are going to your school to get an education. Nowhere is this idea more present than in the rationale for why you have to take exams. Simply put, professors want to see that you are: 1) studying and 2) learning. The only way for them to do this in a setting where they can put everyone in the class on equal footing is to give an exam.

For example, at least in theory, professors could monitor their students' learning by assigning papers to write. But, as we've said before, professors aren't stupid people. They know that if they make a student's grade solely contingent on a paper, students will choose one specific element of the course and focus on it. In other words, students will ignore the rest of the material in the class knowing that their grade is dependent only upon how well they present their narrowly tailored paper. Exams afford professors the opportunity to lock everyone in a room for a specific amount of time and ask them any question they can come up with (presumably, but not always, based on the course material). In this way, professors can assure themselves that everyone has had the same opportunity to study the material and answer the same questions. You may not think so, but in college this masquerades as equality.

Truth be told, it may be the school's administration more than its professors who don't like "paper courses." After all, most professors agree that papers are easier and more interesting to grade (especially if they have 100 students in the class). However, since the primary focus of colleges is to turn out well-educated graduates, school administrators cringe at the idea that students can get credit for a course they only partially understand.

Why do colleges care about the quality of their graduates? Well, it may not be for the philanthropic reasons one might assume. Both private and public colleges are fundamentally businesses concerned with assuring their continuity and success. To meet these goals, schools need to raise money. Ahh, yes, the root of all evil has found its way into higher education. The money that comes into schools in the form of grants and donations is, in part, contingent on the success of students after they leave school. Trust us, the minute they hand you your degree and you're out the door, you'll be flooded by donation requests. Also, colleges attract new students based on their reputation and the success of their graduates. Harvard isn't a prestigious school only because it's got a pretty campus. Students fight to get into Harvard because they expect a quality education and success in their pursuits when they graduate. They expect these things because Harvard graduates have traditionally been successful. All schools are interested in developing this type of reputation, and depend on you, the student, to create it.

So what does all that mean for you? It means that even if professors would like to abolish grading and allow their students to concentrate pressure-free on their own personal edification, it isn't going to happen. Schools set standards that students have to meet in order to get credit for taking a class. These include attendance, a minimum number of classroom hours, and almost always at least one exam. It's appropriate to point out here that in most classes you will have to deal with a combination of exams, short assignments, and papers to fulfill course requirements. Nonetheless, it will be the rare exception, such as a senior seminar class or independent study, where you'll be able to avoid an exam (you'll also get less credit for the course).

This Is An Exam!?

In the fall of 1995, Joe got a call from his little sister, who was in the middle of her first semester at Denison University in Ohio. The conversation went something like this: "My God, Joe, what does this *&%$!!* professor want from me? The question on our first exam was as easy to figure out as Egyptian hieroglyphics, but I wrote down exactly what he taught us. If I can recite the material verbatim, how come I only did okay on the test?" "Ahh, little sister," Joe responded, "you were wise to call the all knowing big brother. Let me explain the answer. Just as the cheetah hunts its prey, so must you pursue the college exam." "Puhleese, Joe, stop being a putz, get a grip and explain this crap to me."

What Joe told his baby sister was simple. Professors don't want you to tell them what they taught you. Now, before you throw the book into the fire, let us explain. In high school you were being taught basic information that every educated person needs to have some understanding of. In college, you continue to learn information, but you also begin to focus on *how to think*. Higher education involves learning how to examine problems, questions, and even answers. No longer are professors simply interested in your understanding of the facts needed to answer a question. In college, professors are testing to see how well you understand the components of the question, analyze the possible answers, and construct an answer.

The best way to illustrate this is by example. Melanie had an exam that read:

Third and Final Exam
English 154
December 16, 1991

Instructions: Be sure that you answer the questions asked. In your discussion be as <u>specific</u> as possible and provide ample evidence (details, examples), as well as page references from the text where necessary, to support your points. The value of your answer depends on the <u>quality</u> of your <u>analyses</u> and <u>arguments</u> and your <u>evidence</u> to support them. If you don't have time to finish an answer in essay form, provide an outline for the remainder of your argument/points and page references, where necessary, for evidence.

ANSWER ONE OF THE FOLLOWING QUESTIONS
(EACH WILL "COUNT" AS ONE EXAM OR AS 25%
OF THE FINAL GRADE):

I. (60 Minutes)

In the last three novels read during the course—*The Crying of Lot 49*, *Realms of Gold*, and *Beloved*—each of the three female protagonists—Oedipa, Frances, and Sethe—contemplates and tries to come to terms with the past in order to deal with the present and the future.

(a) Discuss briefly the nature of the past she contemplates (e.g., specific events, general personal history, family history, world history).

(b) Analyze the effect of the contemplation and attempt to come to terms with the past on her life.

II. Select the three novels read this semester that you found technically the most interesting and rewarding (in terms of structure, point of view, stream of consciousness, patterns of imagery, etc.) and defend the specific reasons for your choices.

Huh? Don't worry, it's not important that we know the material in order to discern what the professor wants here. In fact, this professor, unlike most, has been very gracious in her phrasing of the question, so that it's pretty clear what she is looking for. It's clear from the professor's instructions that if you only tell her what the plots of the books you read were, you're going to fail. Notice, though, that this doesn't mean you can do away with the facts. (In fact, the professor goes so far as to ask for page citations on this exam.) Instead, the professor here is looking for you to analyze the question, construct an argument/answer, and defend it with the facts. The professor hasn't told you in class what a good argument is; in fact, he or she probably doesn't care what you argue. As long as what you say makes sense and is based on fact, you'll do fine (Melanie did). This is a case-in-point example of a professor testing how you think.

The principles illustrated in this example are as applicable to English as they are to Political Science or any essay exam. This analytical way of thinking may be new to many students going into their freshman year. Don't panic. Honestly, it may take you a couple of exams before you get the hang of it. (We'll talk about practice exams later.) The good news is, everybody else is figuring out this new exam-taking strategy also. Since most exams are given on a curve, meaning that you are graded to some extent on how well the other people in the class do, your grade will be fine. Moreover, even if you bomb, remember that professors generally place less importance on exams given in the beginning of the course. It will be your final exam that will be weighed the heaviest in grading, so you'll have a chance to improve your average over the course of the semester. Finally, some professors will even allow you to drop your lowest exam grade because they understand that everyone has a bad day once in a while. Joe's sister was able to do this at Denison and she survived her first semester just fine.

Pick Your Poison: Test Formats

Up until now, we've focused on the essay exam as the professor's test of choice. In fact, we'd take an educated guess that about 90 percent of the exams you'll take in college will be in essay format. Nonetheless, you may occasionally get a short answer exam, a multiple-choice exam, a true-false exam, an oral exam, or a combination of any of these styles.

Short answer exams are designed to test your basic knowledge of the course material. Since professors generally ask for answers only a paragraph or two long, you can't go into great detail in answering these questions. As a result, you need to think about nailing the key ideas quickly. This in and of itself should give you a clue about how to answer short answer questions: your professor is looking for something specific in response to each question. If you find yourself structuring and writing a long theoretical answer, you've missed what the professor wants. If the answer isn't obvious at first, skip the question and come back to it later. Remember, since it's a short answer test there are going to be a bunch of similarly weighted questions. If you have to skip one or two, but get the other fifteen right, you're going to do well.

You've probably taken multiple-choice exams your whole life, so you should have plenty of experience with these. At the very least you had to take the SAT or ACT to get into college, so you've taken at least one grossly unfair and pressure-filled multiple-choice exam. (We like to make fun of standardized testing when we can.) If you were smart, you took The Princeton Review's course or read their test prep materials to get ready for these tests. If you didn't, we, as former TPR site director and teacher, are going to give you a couple of pointers.

First, if all the questions are weighted equally, don't waste time trying to figure out the answer to one question while other easier ones await. Obviously, you get nothing more by getting a hard question right rather than an easier one. Okay, maybe you get some personal satisfaction, but personal satisfaction won't get you into law school.

Next, time yourself on each question so that you can finish the whole test in the time allotted. This is kind of a corollary to the last point. If you're taking too much time, guess what the answer is and move on. Even if you get the first fifty of 100 questions right because you spent time on each answer, leaving the last fifty blank will still give you a big fat F.

Finally, and most importantly, use the process of elimination and *guess*. There is no penalty for guessing on a multiple-choice exam. Think about it! How is your professor going to know that you guessed? He's not. You need to get into the habit of eliminating those answers that you know, for whatever reason, are wrong, and guessing which answer is right. If you want, mark these questions with a star, and if you have time at the end of the test you can come back to them. Otherwise, live with your guesses and go on. Every answer you can eliminate helps you improve your chances of getting the question right (e.g. $\frac{1}{5}$ eliminated = 25 percent chance of getting it right, $\frac{2}{5} = 33\%$, $\frac{3}{5} = 50\%$). Applying this strategy to the whole test will improve your score.

True-false tests are likely to be more difficult than they appear. Come on folks, it's college! The true-false questions are not going to be obvious ones. You're never going to see "True or False: Humans eat food" as a question on an exam. Instead, if your professor has decided to give you a true-false exam, steel yourself for more realistic questions such as: "True or False: F.E.C. regulations passed between 1975 and 1990 have had a more limited impact on the influence of PACs in American congressional elections than they have on American Presidential campaign finance." Even if our sample question seems easy, professors will go further and try to trick you by creating a question that has true and false elements. Remember, for a question to be "true" the entire statement must be true. However, no matter how hard the questions are on the exam, you have a 50 percent chance of getting them right. Once again, *guess!*

Oral exams are usually given as a part of most language classes. Just knowing how to write French won't help you find a bathroom in Paris. Proverbially, you'd be up the Seine without a pencil. Don't let these exams get you upset. Professors don't usually place as much grading weight on oral exams as they do on written tests, and everyone sounds silly saying "Where can I borrow a bicycle pump?" in halting Japanese. Use the language lab if your school has one. Otherwise, pay attention to your professor's accent. It's likely that your professor will appreciate your effort if not your flawless pronunciation.

Finally, the most likely scenario for a college exam is that you'll have a combination of all these testing techniques. We have two tips for you here: 1) Make up a time schedule for the different parts of the test and stick to it and; 2) Do the parts of the test worth the most points first. These points really emphasize what we've explained above. You always want to put yourself in a position to finish the test, and if you have to quickly eliminate and guess, you want it to be on the least weighted parts of the test.

We have one last bit of advice for you to always keep in mind no matter what type of test you're taking. DO NOT PANIC. Panic kills students. If you have to take five minutes to get yourself under control, do it. If you have attended class and studied for the exam, you will do fine. If you think the test is difficult, so does everyone else. You must learn to put panic aside and take the test. We know that this can be difficult to master, but hang in there and you'll get it.

Clue: Colonel Mustard in the Study Hall with a Bic Pen (aka What's on the Exam?)

High school was great in the respect that teachers would usually help you figure out what was going to be on the tests. First of all, the tests were usually often enough so that you could figure out, for example, that since the last test covered up to chapter three, and since you just finished going over chapter six in class, the test was going to be on chapters four, five, and six. Second, for the major exams, teachers would just tell you what was going to be on the test: "World War I and II are not covered on this year's American History exam." This isn't going to happen in college. Your professor is going to expect you to know all of the material covered in the class on your exam. However, if you look carefully, you should be able to find some clues that will help you figure out what to expect on the test.

For example, many courses are developed around themes. If you can recognize the themes, you can guess what you're going to be tested on. For instance, in an English class you may read five or six novels with female lead characters. You can expect to get a question asking you to compare and contrast the qualities of the different characters on your exam. Similarly, in a Political Science class, you may focus on the system of government in several countries. You can expect to be tested on the similarities and differences of the systems and to evaluate which one functions most effectively. Keep in mind that you may not hit the question directly on point. Even if you don't, you'll undoubtedly be able to incorporate the answer you've thought about into the answer for another question.

Another clue to look for is what part of the subject your professor seems to be most interested in. There are lots of ways to do this. For example, if you pay attention to your professor's lectures you may see his academic passion. If every example your professor gives in Economics class involves a Pacific Rim country's economy, that's probably what he's interested in. In some form Pacific Rim economies will show up on the exam. By the way, this is a true example. When Joe was in the Politics Honors seminar at NYU, his professor (who he loved, he'd like to note) always gave examples based on Pacific Rim countries. It turned out that the professor had spent most of his career as an economist and political scientist evaluating such countries. If you find out something like this about your professor, you can look for the influence of his specialty on the exam.

> "Usually our professors have the personality of the subject they teach. Many times it's easier to study the teacher, rather than the topic."
>
> —James Madison University Student

You can also do some basic research to find out what your professor is interested in. For example, try looking up your professor in your school's library system. Many professors write and publish articles and books. If you find out that your Latin professor is a noted authority on ancient church documents, and you touched on that in class, look for it on the exam.

Another giveaway as to what topics your professor may feel are most important are the paper topics he suggests. As we've previously discussed, you'll often have to write a paper and take an exam to fulfill the requirements of a course. If your professor suggests paper topics for the course, you should see if there are any trends in the suggestions. For example, if you're in a Psychology class and two out of every three suggested paper topics deals with children, you can probably guess that this is your professor's specialty. If you focus on child psychology is class, look for it to appear on your exam. Once again, remember that although there's no guarantee that your professor will specifically ask about this on the exam, you'll still be able to use the information in an answer.

We have to write in one caveat. Never, ever, put your eggs all in one basket. If you try to guess what's going to be on the exam and only study for that, you're screwed if you're wrong. Your professor won't be sympathetic when you try to persuade him not to fail you because you knew the answer to a question he didn't ask.

Strategy

Everybody comes to college with a personal system of test taking which they developed in high school. For example, some people don't study the day before the exam, some people underline the important parts of the exam question in pencil, and some people think that eating a big breakfast is they key. We urge you to do what works for you. Nonetheless, we thought we'd discuss some general test-taking strategies.

Okay, let's get this out of the way now: DON'T PANIC! Maintaining your composure is the single most important part of exam strategy. We can't tell you how many people we know that have panicked upon reading an exam question and wasted the first twenty minutes of their time bemoaning their misfortune. Most of these people at some point realize that it's not as bad as they thought because, for example, they didn't read the question carefully. At that point though they've missed the boat and it's all because they panicked.

We know that you, of course, would never do this. However, in case you have a friend who might benefit from the advice, the way to overcome panic is simple. Imagine your professor naked! No, we're kidding about this, but the principle is sound. If you panic when you first get your exam, during the exam, or at its end, just take a minute and relax. Breathe deeply, think about what you're doing after the exam, take a drink (NOT of Scotch), imagine being in Paris, it doesn't matter! The two or three minutes you spend zoning out will be inconsequential compared to the time and energy you'd expend figuring out how to incorporate your imminent F into your GPA. If it helps, just think to yourself that the exam is graded on a curve and that there's a couple of people in the class you know you can outperform. It doesn't matter if it's true or not, as long as it helps you relax. Last but not least, remember that one grade never makes or breaks you. You'll survive no matter how you do on the exam.

Now that that's out of the way, we can turn to more specific advice. One important thing that all students need to do is *carefully read through the exam in its entirety before you start writing*. This is important because many students fail to answer the correct amount of questions and correctly apportion their time so as to finish the whole exam. An exam can seem awfully long and unfair when you answer all three essay questions on the test rather that the two out of three that the professor asked for. When you read the whole test carefully, you'll also be able to figure out which questions to approach first. As we've discussed before, you want to do the questions worth the most first. If all questions are equal, it doesn't make a difference which one you do first, but at least you know what to expect.

If there's some material you're worried about remembering, perhaps a list or a formula, *look it over right before you go into the exam, and jot it down in the margin of your test or your blue book as soon as you sit down*. This handy little technique means you only have to remember the tough bit of information for a couple of minutes.

Another important bit of strategy: *outline each question before you start writing*. We don't mean that you should spend twenty minutes writing an expansive outline. That would be just as silly as panicking. Instead, take two or three minutes to jot down where you want to go with your answer. This will help you organize your answer so that you remember what you want to say and will keep you on track so you don't drift off and write things you don't need to (see below for more on this). Professors love clear, concise, and organized answers. A brief outline will help you write one.

As we alluded to above, it's essential that you *answer the right question.* You're probably thinking that we've lost it, but don't worry, we're cool. You'd be surprised how many students answer the question that they want to answer, as opposed to the one the professor wrote. This is probably a product of a student studying hard, but learning some things better than others. After all, it's only natural to want to put your best foot forward. Nonetheless, professors won't be thrilled by a brilliantly crafted answer to a question other than the one they wrote.

When you start writing you should *write on every other line.* This may seem like a waste of paper, and it probably is, but it serves two important functions. First, an exam written on every other line is easier on the professor's eyes to read, especially if yours happens to be the fiftieth one he's picked up that day. No matter what you have to say, if your professor gets frustrated because he can't read it or skips stuff because it's all beginning to blend together on the page, your grade will suffer as a result. Second, writing on every other line allows you to go back to a specific part of the exam and add things or make corrections. This way you won't have lines drawn to your answers, things crossed out or pages torn out of your test. Your professor will appreciate your organization.

Also, if you have time you should *read over your answers before you hand in your exam.* This bit of strategy doesn't need much explanation. If you read your answers before you hand the exam in you'll be able to find and correct the tiny little mistakes everyone makes in the heat of battle. You'd be surprised how many points you can lose on a test with just a few "do's" written out as "do not's" or when you get the names of the characters in a book mixed up.

If you incorporate these simple suggestions into the techniques you've developed through your high school test-taking experience, you'll be ready to rock your exams! Good luck.

Cheating

Quite frankly, we think it sucks to have to write about this. Really, we're not uptight ethicists, but we're going to sound like it for a bit. We also going to try and put the fear of death in you so you never cheat.

First, if you cheat you're going to get caught. You might get caught by the professor who has read enough exams to recognize what college students are capable of. You might get caught by another student in the class who correctly feels that he's getting shafted because you're butchering the curve or because he studied for seven straight days and he doesn't even feel comfortable with the material. You might even get caught by someone with nothing to lose by you cheating at all, but who'd love to even the score for something you once said or did. No matter what, you're going to get caught.

When you get caught there will be "nowhere to run to baby, and nowhere to hide." Forget that line you've heard about some professors feeling sorry for students who get caught cheating and not wanting to ruin their lives. Nice try. Most colleges structure it so that even if the professor wants to give you a second chance, she's got her hands tied. Colleges do this by imposing punishments on professors who fail to report cases of cheating. Even so, it's more likely that your professor will take your actions as a personal affront to his dignity and professionalism and be the first one in line to prosecute you. Try getting a job recommendation from this professor!

Furthermore, your school will be looking to make an example of you. The fact is that cheating happens in college and lots of people get away with it. As a result, when a school catches one of its students cheating, they take a real hard stand, hoping to send a message to the rest of the morally bereft members of the student body. Put succinctly, you'll be hoping that all the school does is bounce your tail out of there. They might decide to put a permanent mark on your transcript indicating that you were disciplined for cheating. Then, after they help you pack your bags, you'll have an ice cube's chance in hell of getting into another respectable college.

Mom and Dad will always love you, right? Yes, they'll love you, but they'll never be more disappointed than when the Dean of Students calls to tell them you're on your way home. You'll just lie to your parents, right? Wrong. The school will put together a documented file for your parents and anyone else who's interested that will include how, what, when, where, and why you cheated. If your parents are helping you pay for college, they also won't be ecstatic about the fact that your stupidity just flushed their $20,000 down the crapper. Yes, that's right, there are no refunds available for mandatorily expelled students. On that note, if you took loans out, they're immediately payable when your school notifies the lender of their disciplinary action.

That's not enough? Fine, let's talk about your life plans after cheating. For example, take one likely scenario. Your college expels you and marks your permanent transcript (which they will undoubtedly do), but you're able to find some classless college that will let you get your degree. No higher education awaits you, our ethic-less friend. No law school, medical school, or business school will touch you. Even if you got in to law school, for example, the State Bar Committee on Ethics wouldn't let you within a nautical mile of a license.

You get the picture. It's not worth getting a B over a C in French Poetry, when you could potentially be subjecting yourself to a life of asking people, "Can I refill your drink?" Cheaters are losers in life. Thank God we know our readers don't cheat.

GRADES: WHAT THEY ARE AND WHY THEY MATTER

We'd like to use this space to tell you that it's not what shows up on your report card that counts, it's how much your experiences enrich you as a person. Unfortunately, this would be a big fat lie. Grades do count. They count for a lot. To take it to the most basic level, you can't graduate if you don't get at least passing grades. But merely passing is far from good enough. To make college worthwhile you need to get good grades. Although we've told you that you don't need to choose a major your freshman year, that doesn't mean you don't have to worry about your grades. Particularly since you don't know where your academic road may take you, you need to keep all your options open. If you decide to go to graduate school—even if you make the decision two years after you graduate—your college transcript will play a big part in the admissions process. Many employers will also look at your grades, because you don't have a long job history to prove to them what a good worker you are. Why pay thousands of dollars a year for your education if what ends up on your transcript won't get you a job or get you into graduate school?

GPA

Your grades for your first year are also important because they lay the foundation for your grade point average (GPA). This average is the numerical equivalent of your letter grades. Most colleges use a four-point scale, so to figure out your GPA, you assign points to each of your grades as follows:

A = 4 points
B = 3 points
C = 2 points
D = 1 point
F = absolutely no points

If you have a plus or a minus letter grade, add or subtract .33. A B+ would be a 3.33; a B- a 2.67.

Next, you multiply the points for each class by the number of credit hours the class is worth (this is the number of hours the class meets each week), for example:

Class	Grade =	Points ×	Credit Hours =	Total Points
Intro to Brain Surgery	A	4	6	24
Organic Chemistry	B	3	6	18
French Poetry	C	2	4	08
Victorian Literature	D	1	3	03
Dancing for Credit	F	0	2	00
Total			21	53

Finally, divide your total points (53) by your total number of credit hours (21) to get your GPA, in this case a 2.523. This would be a pretty solid C average . . . average indeed.

When we say your grades freshman year are the foundation of your GPA, it's because you never get a clean slate again. You do get a new GPA each semester, but all of your semester GPAs get averaged together to create what's known as your cumulative GPA, often just called your "cum." And it's your cum that's most important to grad schools and employers. As your points for various semesters add up, individual classes have less of an impact on the large number of total points, so it gets harder and harder to make a significant change in your cumulative GPA. This is great if you start out with a 3.7, but if you start with a 2.0, it's going to take a lot of hard work to bring it up.

We should also point out that, as evidenced by the example above, classes that have the most credit hours also have the most impact on your GPA. Thus, it doesn't take a rocket scientist to figure out that you should give priority to the higher credit classes. If, after all of our warnings, you still procrastinate and end up having to choose which class you get the work done for, remember which class will count more in the end.

Before you panic because you think that you're doomed to a life of drudgery if you blow your GPA your first semester, do yourself a favor and take a deep breath. Many, many students have trouble their first semester. College courses are a whole new ball game, and college professors are often stingy with good grades. Colleges are also selective in their admissions: if you were a top student in your high school class, it's very possible that many of your classmates were also the cream of the crop. Racking up the As is not going to be easy, so don't be too hard on yourself if it takes you a semester to get into the swing of things. And remember, we said it would take a lot of hard work to pull up an initially low GPA; we didn't say it wasn't possible.

"When they told us that not everyone could be at the top of the class, we all thought, 'Gee that must be hard for some people.' Now I realize that I'm one of those people."

—Rice University Student

Take Joe, for instance. He was promising student all through high school, but decided to tackle a pre-med major his freshman year of college. (You remember Joe, he's the one who's in law school now.) A couple of dismal grades in his science classes convinced him to change his major, but not before he had a pretty sorry GPA on his hands. Well, as evidenced by the fact that he not only got into a great graduate school, but has done well academically there, Joe survived and even thrived despite his initial tangle with the numbers.

Joe's saga is also a good illustration of another reason why you shouldn't panic. Graduate schools and employers do look at your cumulative GPA first, but they also look at the GPA you earned in your major. This is a separate GPA that is based only on the courses you take for your major; so if you did a good job of choosing a major it will be pretty high. Your major GPA is usually a good indication of your abilities, because it's based on work you did as a more mature and seasoned student. In the process of trying out courses in different subjects, Joe discovered his affinity for Political Science. This time he not only loved the topic, he was damn good at it. And, not surprisingly, law schools were much more interested in his 3.8 Political Science average than in the fact that he lowered his cum by bombing Chemistry 101 his freshman year. It may take a little hit and miss for you to find your specialty, but you *will* find it. Just another good reason to shop around the departments before you zero in on a major.

Dangerous Curves

Grade point averages aren't the only grading experience that may be new to you in college. This may also be your first encounter with the forced curve. This can work one of two ways. In the first case, a professor decides that the grades in the class will fit into a bell curve pattern. This assumes the bulk of the class (the hump of the curve) does average work and gets Cs. The remainder of the grades are also distributed on the slope of the curve, with next largest portion of the class split between Bs and Ds, and the smallest portion of the class split evenly between As and Fs. This means that even if everyone gets a 90 or above, the people with the lowest 90s still get an F. Fun, huh? This kind of curve can create nasty tension in a class, not only because everyone wants to win the top percentages, but also because there's a tendency to resent the students who outscore everyone to set the top of the curve. If you think this kind of curve is harsh, listen to the second kind. In this case, the professor decides ahead of time what the percentage cut-off will be for each letter grade. So if the top score in the class was a 75, and the professor had decided that a 76 was the cut-off to get a C, everyone in the class will get a D or an F. On the brighter side, if the professor decides that anything over a 90 is an A, it's possible that the entire class could get As.

Pass/Fail

Pass/fail is another grading option that you probably haven't encountered before. Grading may actually be a bad term to use in this explanation, because you don't get a letter grade if you take a class pass/fail. Just as it sounds, as long as you get above an F you pass the course and get the credits. An F is still an F: You fail and get no credits. Before you get too excited, we'll tell you right now that you can't use the pass/fail option for all of your classes. In fact, you'll probably take few or no pass/fail classes. This is true for several reasons. Some professors won't allow students to take their classes pass/fail, because they feel it takes away the motivation to work hard. Many schools don't allow students to take required courses pass/fail, because your performance in these courses is considered an essential part of earning your degree. Plus, even if you can take a class pass/fail, a P on your transcript is far less impressive to a graduate school or employer than a good letter grade is. Too many Ps and anyone who looks at your transcript will label you a slacker.

You're probably wondering why the pass/fail option exists if there are all of these reasons why you can't or shouldn't use it. Well, there are a few exceptions. For instance, maybe you've always wanted to make pottery or learn to play tennis. You can probably take an art or physical education class to do either of these things, but what if you discover that you are *far* from being a budding artisan or the next Martina Navratilova? You don't want to lower your GPA just because you decided to try something new. This is the perfect time to use pass/fail. If the class in question bares no relation to your career aspirations, it probably won't matter to grad schools or employers if you take a P for the course.

Incompletes

The last grading practice we want to explain to you is taking an "incomplete" for a course, which, hopefully, you will never do. If, due to some extreme circumstances, you can't complete the work for a course, particularly a final paper or exam, by the end of the semester, a professor can give you an incomplete (I) instead of failing you. To get rid of the incomplete, you have to finish the required work by a certain date. If you don't meet this extended deadline, you fail the course. If it's given for legitimate reasons, an incomplete can be an academic lifesaver, giving you the time you need to complete your work. However, if you don't handle an incomplete responsibly, it can hurt you as much as it could have helped you. If you're not conscientious about finishing the outstanding work as soon as possible, it can turn into a nightmare. You may find it hard to focus on a class once the semester is officially over. No one else is writing papers or studying for exams, and you won't want to either. And if you put things off for too long, it will start conflicting with the work for your new classes. Take our word for it: it's probably worth working overtime and finishing on time if there's any way you can. It may be a pressure-filled end of the semester, but you'll be glad when it's over that everything is finished and you can get on with your life.

Why Grades Matter

We've talked a lot about grades, and it's probably just about time we moved on. *But* (there's always a but) before we do, we'll reiterate why it is that you have to worry about grades in the first place. While it's always nice to live for the present, it's never a good idea to forget the future, and grades, like it or not, affect your future. If you want to go to graduate school or get a job—and we're betting that one of these things is in your plans—you need a good transcript. Employers and schools may in fact take you based solely on your dazzling personality, but just in case there's any competition, you want the grades to back you up.

It is also possible, or even probable, that you may change your mind about what you want to do somewhere down the road. If you blow off your studies now because you have no intention of going to graduate school, how will you feel five years from now when you realize you really want or need an MBA? Or what if you concentrate on your French classes, sometimes to the detriment of your other courses, because you're sure you want to be a high school French teacher? That could be a problem if you decide that all high school students are extremely annoying and you want to get accepted into a Ph.D. program so you can teach college. These examples may be too distant to seem relevant. Grades can matter sooner than you think. What if there's an honors program in your major, but you have to have a high overall GPA to get into it? What if tuition goes up next year, or your financial aid package decreases? If you ever have to compete for scholarship funds, you want grades that will keep you in the running. No matter how set and secure the future seems, do yourself a favor and make sure your grades won't let you down— no matter what.

STRESS

So what do you get when you combine all of this academic pressure, all of the adjustments you're making to your new life at school, and maybe even a little tension with your roommate? Stress! A little stress isn't necessarily a bad thing. As we said earlier, many people don't get motivated until there's some pressure to perform. However, if you're spending a lot of time worrying, or you feel like there's no way you can get everything done, your stress has passed an acceptable level.

Stress is often the result of feeling like you've lost control: You can't finish all of the papers you have due; you can't understand anything your Calculus professor is saying; you can't deal with your roommate's living habits; etcetera. So to conquer the stress you have to take action—put yourself back in the driver's seat. The mistake most people make is thinking that they have to come up with a plan that solves everything instantly. If we could tell you how to do that, you'd be watching infomercials filmed at our Hawaiian estate. Here are a few suggestions for getting out from under what feels like a mountain of stress:

- **Make lists.** You feel like you have so many things to do that you don't know where to start. Well, start by writing everything down, and we mean *everything*. From writing a ten-page paper to doing your laundry, put everything on the list. Then prioritize. If you have an exam tomorrow morning, put it at the top of the list. Thinking of a topic for the paper that's due in four days is important, but it can wait until after the exam. Likewise, reading for tomorrow afternoon's class is a good idea, but doing well on the test is more important. Once everything is on the list, focus only on the top item. Put two through ten out of your mind; you have the list to remind you of them once you've done number one.

- **Know your limits.** Freshman year may not be the time to take more than the standard number of credits a semester. Likewise, it may be overly optimistic to think you can handle your first semester of pre-med while playing on the varsity lacrosse team and running for class president. Melanie tried taking sixteen credits, acting in a play, and working at the bookstore and found, quite reasonably of course, that she'd just have to give up sleeping for the semester (yeah, that worked *really* well). Starting college is exciting, and there are lots of opportunities, but you can't do everything at once. If the lists you're making are thirty items long, maybe you should think about cutting back on how much you're taking on. Maybe you should give up one of your extracurricular activities, or there's a class that you could drop and take another semester.

- **All work and no play . . .** It's easy to think that the solution to your stress is to work non-stop, night and day, to get everything done. Wrong. If you do nothing but work, you will be exhausted, depressed, and even more stressed out. You need to build some fun and relaxation into your schedule, no matter how busy you are. Taking some time to hang out with a friend, or even taking a nap, will help you keep a positive attitude when you go back to work.

- **Take good care of yourself.** This is your mother talking. Try to eat at least a couple of vegetables a day, even if it's just peppers on your pizza. Get some exercise and get some sleep. If you don't take care of yourself, your busy schedule will take its toll quickly.

- **Get help.** This sounds more dramatic than it is. Your school probably offers many services to help students through their four years. Possibilities include:

  - **Tutors:** If you have trouble with a particular subject, look into getting a tutor. A few one-on-one study sessions and someone to look over your assignments can make a big difference.

  - **Writing Centers:** Many schools have centers that are staffed with people who can proofread your writing, help you sharpen your research skills, work with you to develop a thesis, and generally ensure that your paper-writing skills improve. Even if there's no formal center, most professors, teaching assistants, and librarians are more than willing to help you.

  - **Professors:** Take advantage of office hours or make an appointment to talk to your professor. As a general rule, professors are happy to help. However, they don't like to feel like you're wasting their time. For instance, it's fine to think of a couple of paper topics and make an appointment with your professor to discuss which one you should use. It's not a good idea to plop down in her office and tell her you have no ideas and were hoping she'd pick a topic for you.

  - **Residence Life Staff:** We've already discussed how your R.A. can be helpful. If your stress is due to your living situation, this is the way to go.

  - **Counseling Center:** The counselors who work at colleges are experts in helping students deal with everything from insomnia to exam anxiety. If nothing you try seems to be reducing your stress level, you shouldn't feel bad about talking to a counselor. You're the reason they're there, and your visits will be completely confidential.

Hopefully your stressed-out periods will be few and far between, and our suggestions will help you out when you hit them. By the way, stress is no freshman phenomenon. You'll have to deal with it for the next sixty or seventy years. Consider developing your stress-management techniques as a long-term investment.

CHAPTER 6

Papers

THIS IS NOT A BOOK REPORT

In chapter five, we talked about how your professors would be looking for a higher level of analysis in your exam essay answers. The same thing holds true for what professors want to see in a college paper.

In high school you probably wrote most of your papers for English or History classes. The topics were usually fairly straightforward. You might have written "A Comparison of World Wars" or "Charles Dickens' Stories." Either way, your teachers were looking to see that you had basic research skills and that you had actually read some stuff. They never encouraged you to tell them what you thought on a subject; they might have even discouraged "opinion writing." This will change in college.

In college, professors will assume that your high school teachers made sure that you could read and spit back what happened in a book. They won't want to see that. Your professors will be looking, as in your exam answers, for some in-depth analysis and some unique comments on the issues raised in your paper.

Professors expect this, in part, because they let you choose your paper topics. After all, the reasoning goes, you chose to take their class, you chose your paper topic, so it's rational to expect you to have something to say in your paper. This is good for the student in many respects. It liberates you to write papers that actually interest you. Novel concept, huh? Also, it lets you express your feelings and ideas on a particular point. It could be that you want to write a paper on the incredible similarities between President Bill Clinton's economic policy and the ability of Puxatawny Phil, the groundhog, to predict the length of winter. Perhaps you feel that John Grisham novels illustrate the same qualities that make Shakespeare's plays so unique. It really doesn't matter, your professor will let you try and write on these topics. But she's going to expect you to have something to say.

The fact that professors are going to expect something more than a book report from you means that you actually have to think about your paper topic. Professors are usually willing to help students come up with a good topic. In fact, many professors will require that you have them approve your paper topic and submit a paper proposal well before the end of the course so they know that you haven't forgotten to start working.

We're going to talk about research later on, but keep in mind now that when you're trying to decide on a paper topic you should do some preliminary research to ensure that there's something to write on. For example, no matter how fascinating you think an analysis and comparison of Reese's Pieces to Reese's Peanut Butter Cups would be, if there's no authority to support your position you can't write your paper on it. (Anyway, it's obvious that the crunchy shell ruins the whole peanut butter to chocolate ratio.) Preliminary research is especially important before you go to see your professor about your paper topic. It's a bummer to have your professor tell you that you're the only one who has ever considered such a trivial issue worth writing a paper on.

On a final note, don't worry if your paper-writing skills take some time to develop. The transition between a high school book report and a college paper is a difficult one to make. Just remember, if you put thought into choosing a topic, do some basic research, and then present an analytical paper you'll be on the right track.

Research

Well, now that we've established that you have to have something to say, we can explain that you also have to have something to back it up. Trust us, it's not that we don't think that you're fully capable of writing a paper solely on your opinion. We know you can, and when you're a Ph.D. you probably will. Ahh, and just think we'll have known you when . . . For now though, you need to have some outside authority to back up your proposition. By way of analogy, you might think of writing a paper as having an argument with a friend. Your argument is always stronger when you can say "Yeah, Bill, I understand that you think that your 1975 El Camino is the best performing car in history. Unfortunately, *Consumer Reports* this month seems to disagree." Similarly, in doing research for your paper, your goal is to find outside support for your position.

We're both twenty-five, but we feel old in this respect: Research techniques have gotten incredibly more sophisticated even since we graduated college. Never before have there been more options available to college students than today. Not only do you have your traditional library resources such as books, newspapers, magazines, journals, and microfilm, but you have online research series such as Lexis/Nexis, America Online, CompuServe, Prodigy, Encarta, and the rest. Today, you can sit in your dorm room and have access to virtually every bit of information recorded by mankind. Look, we know how to use all this stuff, but even we think it's pretty cool. Our grandparents got their information from one daily newspaper, and we get upset if we can't get the editorials for the French daily newspaper *Le Monde* before lunch.

So what does all this mean for you? We've got good news and bad news. The bad news first. More than ever professors are going to expect thoroughly researched papers from their students. Professors now look for students to use a variety of different sources to help state their position. Furthermore, since professors have the same access to information as students, they can easily check on the degree of research you did by simply seeing what they can find on a Nexis sweep. For example, your professor will not be pleased with you if Nexis tells them that the *New York Times* ran a twenty-part series supporting your position and you quote the same edition of the *Washington Post* all throughout your paper. You're going to have to do good research to get a good grade.

Now for the good news. Doing good research is easy with all the tools available to students today. You have no excuse for failing to get all the pertinent information on a particular topic. Don't get us wrong. Not every paper needs or should have every piece of available information crammed into its annals. (*Annals*. Not what you thought. Sick mind.) However, let us tell you that it's going to be real impressive to your professor if you can write:

Although the Feb. 18, 1992 *San Francisco Chronicle* editorial strongly disagrees with the proposition that all blah blahs are blah blahs, a recent release by the Russian news agency "Tass" suggests that all blah blahs may, in fact, be blah blahs. The Russian sentiment is echoed by a recent policy memo circulated by the World Bank, as reported in the January 20, 1995, issue of the *Financial Times.*

Okay, we know that this example is a little ludicrous. The point is valid though. The fact that you covered a West Coast daily, a Russian news agency, and a Wall Street trade paper will win you big points with your professor. (For the record, you'd better footnote all of this, but we'll talk about this later.) The best thing is that you could do all this research during a commercial in the David Letterman show! This makes a paper fun to write.

A lot of how you structure your research is going to be dictated by the resources you have at your disposal. For example, your school may or may not be connected to the online services we mentioned. (You should be if possible!) Here are a couple of general tips to help you get started:

- **Go to your library's database and do a subject search.** Almost all libraries these days have computerized databases. In addition to being able to search by author and title, you can usually search by subject. Doing so will provide you with a preliminary idea of what books your library has on your subject.

- **Pick a prominent author in the field and run his name through the computer.** Hopefully, you'll turn up three or four books he's written. If you're lucky, he will have compiled a bibliography in support of his book. This should give you a good idea of the prominent books in the field. Note, though, that you must go look up the books and figure out if they support your position. For one thing, sometimes a bibliography is just plain wrong. For another thing, some writers cite an authority that doesn't directly support the proposition. Finally, you must do your own work.

Stealing a bibliography is plagiarism and very different from using it as a research tool.

- **Do a periodical search.** Even this you can usually do through a database and by subject. This should give you a good idea of what newspapers and "consecutively paginated journals" have said on your topic. As a general rule, the more recent the article, the more effective the citation.

- **If you can, go online.** We've talked about this.

- **Ask your professor.** Remember, the paper topic you're writing on has to deal with the course. Since your professor is a specialist in the topic, who better to ask? Your professor should have a good idea of what's out there, and he or she will appreciate the interest you're showing in the course. This is probably not a good suggestion if the paper is due the next day.

Good research makes for a good paper. Put the time in before you write and you'll be rewarded later!

Structure

So, you know what point you're trying to make and you have tons of valuable information to back it up. It's still important to present your ideas in the right way. What follows is a very general structure of what we feel is a good paper.

At the beginning you should have an introductory paragraph which lays out the reason you're writing the paper. You might call this your "topic paragraph." The point here is to orient the reader and to provide a backdrop for everything that's about to come. This paragraph can be as long or short as necessary. Just be sure that the paragraph answers the question: "Why am I reading this?"

Now you're ready to present your background. Presumably there is something the reader needs to know in order to understand the argument you will present later in the paper. You can't just launch into an argument without setting the stage. To that end, this part of your paper may be more like a book report. You may feel that the reader needs to know the characters in the books you're going to compare or the basic principles of Darwinian theory. Now is your chance to provide the reader with the necessary mini-education they need to comprehend your points. Be careful here though. Don't let this section run on and on because you've failed to boil down all the information you know to the essential points the reader needs to know. In most papers you're not trying to make the reader an expert on the topic. Most new college paper writers botch this and turn their papers into book reports.

After you've laid the foundation for your paper, you're ready to present your arguments. It's almost universally accepted that you need to have at least three main points in support and one point which criticizes your argument. This is true for even the shortest paper. For longer papers you'll want to have two more support points for every contrary point. It's up to you how to place these arguments in your paper. We think it's always a good idea to lead and finish strong. As a result, if we had three arguments in support and one against our argument, we'd organize them by putting our second strongest point first then our weakest point, then the critical point, then conclude with our strongest argument.

Why should you put a critical point in your paper? Good question. Placing a critical point in your paper serves two functions. First, it shows that you understand and have thought about the other side of the argument. Educated people understand that there are many different sides to most arguments, even though they believe their position to be correct. Second, it basically lets you tee up the opposition so your strongest point can knock them out of the ball park. That's why we place our strongest point after the critical point. It looks great when you can write that although the other side has said X the rest of the Western world has accepted that it's definitely Y.

After the brilliant presentation of your arguments, you're ready to conclude. It may be the lawyer in Joe, but he looks at this as an opportunity to present your best case. To be specific, throw objectivity out the window. Hopefully, up to this point in the paper you've fairly presented your arguments and supporting citations and the reader now sees your point. Now's the time to put 'em away! The conclusion is your chance to state the facts as you would have everyone see them. Try to be persuasive and emphasize your key points. Don't mention the opposition if you can help it. If you feel you have no choice, make sure the mention is incidental and not accusatory. You don't want to appear that you're waffling on your points or that you're a sore winner. Comments like "and besides, if the guy who wrote that article isn't a convicted felon, he should be" should not appear in your conclusion.

In conclusion, part of a successful paper comes from the individuality of the author. We urge you to incorporate your own style of writing into your papers. No one set format will always be correct or guarantee an A paper. However, if you concentrate on making a clear and concise argument, grounded in fact and supported by persuasive authority, you'll be off to a good start.

Citation (How Not to Plagiarize)

Don't worry, we're not going to give you a reprise of our cheating speech. However, we do need to discuss a more insidious type of campus scourge. Plagiarism occurs when one deliberately or inadvertently appropriates the words, ideas, or theories of another. You must have heard of this in high school. If you are stupid enough to go out and deliberately plagiarize, go read our section on cheating. It's our experience, though, that most people plagiarize because they don't understand how and when to cite a source. In this part of the chapter we'll help you avoid becoming one of those unwitting but equally guilty plagiarizers.

First, we need to discuss what a citation is. There are many different forms of citation and there is more than one way of correctly citing a proposition. You undoubtedly had to create a bibliography in high school. For example, one way of citing this book would be: Melanie and Joseph C. Sponholz, *The College Companion,* (New York: Random House, 1996). The key here is to cite consistently. This means that you follow the same style of citation and that you cite in the same form. This means that whether you've decided to footnote your paper, endnote your paper, create a bibliography, or do all three, you have to do it in the same way. It would be better to get every one of your citations wrong than to keep changing the way you write them.

Luckily, you don't have to figure this all out on your own. There are a number of excellent guides available for you to use. We have to admit, we used one to make sure that our sample bibliography citation was correct. We actually used two different citation guides when we were in college. Melanie used Joseph Gibaldi and Walter

S. Achert, *MLA Handbook for Writers of Research Papers* (New York: The Modern Language Association of America, 1988). Joe used Kate L. Turabian, *A Manual for Writers of Term Papers, Theses, and Dissertations* (Chicago and London: The University of Chicago Press, 1987). There are also a number of other excellent guides available to you. Pick one and use it consistently. We concede that they aren't the easiest things to use. Sometimes, out of necessity, the explanations can be difficult to understand. Trust us though, once you get in the habit of using one, you'll figure it out. Plus, you only have to memorize one system.

The best advice we can give you to avoid plagiarism is that you can almost never overdo your citation. Specifically, if you ever ask yourself whether or not you should cite something, you should. This is so important that we will say it one time differently: The only things that shouldn't be cited are those that are common knowledge or your own opinion. Even then, you might want to suggest in a citation that many people agree that what you're citing is common knowledge, or that many people support or disagree with your opinion. For example, if you're writing a chemistry paper and you write a sentence that says, "Water molecules are comprised of two hydrogen molecules and one oxygen molecule," you probably don't have to cite it. Everyone who has taken high school chemistry knows that water is H_2O. On the other hand, it certainly wouldn't be incorrect to put a citation in that points out who first figured this out and when. Of course, in our example above, we made it a fairly simple call as to whether or not you need a cite. Sometimes it will be harder to discern when a citation is appropriate, so we'll boil it down for you. Right now, you're probably not an expert on anything you're going to learn in college. If you were you wouldn't be going to school in the first place. As a result, cite everything. Professors dig it, and you won't ever be penalized for it.

Another Note About Procrastination

We've mentioned this topic a couple of times throughout the book, but it deserves repetition here. Procrastination will kill your paper! Everyone, including ourselves, believes that they can "knock out" a paper in whatever time they have left. For example, we know we could've written this book during half-time of the Penn State football game. *Not.* (Go Big Blue!) The reality of the matter is that you probably could knock out a paper in two or three hours. Unfortunately for you, you'd fail that course. Writing papers in college takes research, development, writing and, yes it's true, the dreaded rewriting. You can't correctly write a college paper in a limited amount of time.

There will always be people who started doing their research and writing before you. This doesn't always mean that they're going to do better than you, especially if you start working on your paper with a reasonable amount of time left. However, if you try to write your paper the night before it's due, you've missed the pack and you'll never catch up. If you don't procrastinate, you'll never have to worry about this.

It's Better to Look Good Than To. . .

Our final note on papers should be obvious to everyone. Presentation is a major part of your grade. Make every effort to hand in a readable, neat, and organized paper.

One of the most common faux pas committed by students is a failure to proofread. As a result, they butcher punctuation, spelling, and paragraph structure. No one is perfect. (We're certainly not; that's why we have an editor. (Ed. Note: Who, of course, is perfect.)) If you go back over your paper before you hand it in, you'll improve your grade.

Since you're going to be writing all your papers on a computer and in a program such as WordPerfect or Microsoft Word, there is no excuse for misspelled words. Sure, the occasional "there" when you meant to write "their" is going to creep in. But you should never have total misspellings. We'd give you an example except WordPerfect would correct it. Moreover, since it's so easy to cut and paste pieces of a paper using these computer programs, you should never hand in a paper that isn't completely neat and organized. We've both seen colleagues write in changes to sentence changes or write "see page 3 for explanation" at the top of page eight. If they wanted the explanation at page eight they should have moved it there. We'd be willing to wager that their grade suffered for it.

Finally, we both know people who will play the margins and spacing game to make their paper seem longer or shorter to meet a page limit. Don't do this crap. Here's a clue, folks, professors know that this goes on. They recognize it immediately. How do you think your professor's going to react to you trying to pull the wool over her eyes? If you need to make your paper longer at the last minute, do some spot research or just leave it a couple of lines short. P.S., don't B.S. to make your paper longer; professors will see through that right away, too. If you need to make your paper shorter, there is always something you can cut. Work within the guidelines the professor suggested and you'll get the grade you deserve.

CHAPTER 7

Having A Life

THE BALANCING ACT

Don't let anyone tell you that having fun isn't one of the central purposes of going to college. Yes, you are there to get that all-important B.A., but you're also there to make a lot of friends, have a lot of great times, and, in the process, learn a lot about yourself. Your friends and the times you spend with them will be what you treasure the most about your college years—sappy, but true. The time you spend establishing new relationships and pursuing new interests is just as important as the time you put into your studies. You cannot, we repeat, cannot, study and work all of the time. You will lose your mind. Balance is the key. Giving yourself enough play time will give you the energy and motivation you need to work hard when it's time to buckle down. What you choose to do will be as individual as you are, but in this chapter we'll try to give you an idea of what your options are.

PARTYING

We didn't put partying at the beginning of this chapter by accident. Parties are a *big* part of the social scene at almost every college, particularly on weekends (which can start as early as Wednesday night in college!). From your early experiences with alcohol to the evolution of your love life, a lot of pretty significant events will be tied in some way to parties, so we want to fill you in. We also noticed anywhere we tried to read about partying, all we found were some really basic admonitions about not drinking too much, and you've probably been hearing that advice for years already. We'll talk all about alcohol in a few pages, and we have more to say about it than telling you not to drink. Here we want to discuss the many facets of the party . . .

"Students here work hard through the week, and play hard on the weekends."

—*Wittenberg University Student*

In the Mix

One of the best reasons to go to parties is that they're great places to meet new people. You may think that since you know the person or people who are hosting the party that you'll know everyone there, but this will rarely, if ever, be the case. Information about the party starts out in one circle of friends, but it quickly moves out through friends of friends, friends of friends of friends, random people who overhear the friends conversations, and friends of the random people—you get the idea. Plus, one of the cool parts of college parties is that most of the time anyone is welcome to drop in. If you're in the area (meaning you walk by), you're a potential guest. Part of the excitement of arriving at a party is that you never know what you'll find in the social mix. You meet many of your friends and significant others in class or clubs, but there may be some great people that you don't run into in your daily schedule. There are a lot of problems that arise from excessive drinking, and we're not advocating pounding beers before a party, *but* many people do get over their shyness after a couple of beers, making striking up a conversation with complete strangers a distinct possibility. Anyway, if you always party with only your small group of friends, your group isn't going to get bigger very quickly.

In some less frequent instances, you may go to a party and realize pretty quickly that the mix is not one you're interested in being part of. Maybe there's so much drinking going on that you'd be lucky to find anyone capable of finishing a sentence, much less carrying on a conversation. Maybe alcohol isn't the only drug being used (we'll talk more about that later too). Or maybe you're the only non-varsity athlete, the only one who wasn't part of the play that just closed, etcetera. If this happens, don't freak out and decide that you're a social misfit. Move on, and chances are that within the hour you'll be with a different group of people having a great time.

High Drama

For some reason (actually for several reasons) emotions run high at parties. It may start out as a fun and mellow evening, but by the end of the night chances are there's a blow-up fight, a traumatic break-up, a hook-up that sets the gossip mill churning, or some equally ridiculous situation that has someone crying, someone yelling, and doors slamming. First, realize that no matter how intense the situation seems at that moment it will most likely seem irrelevant by brunch tomorrow. This is doubly important to remember if you're the one in tears or on the verge of slamming the door.

Alcohol is the culprit in many of these mini soap operas. People use their inebriation as an excuse to do all kinds of really stupid stuff. The most popular soap episode could be dubbed "The Hook-up," and there are several common scripts that result from the combination of drinking and lots of women meeting lots of men. One typical scene involves two women or two men (often friends or acquaintances) who know they are both attracted to the same person. At the beginning of the night, when everyone is sober and reasonable, this is no problem. However as the evening and the alcohol progress, someone makes a move, someone is infuriated, and everyone is embroiled in the night's high drama. In typical scene number two, a couple comes to the party together and one of them leaves with someone else, resulting in the expected blow-out, break-up, etcetera. Typical scenario three has two random unattached people hook-up at a party. Sounds fine, but inevitably one of them returns to the party telling tales (we won't be sexist and say who this is), and the other is humiliated. You may be deciding right now that you're not going to any parties: That resolution will last for about twenty minutes. Okay, so you just won't drink: Easier said than done. Your last argument is that you'd never be one of the soap opera actors described above: Don't bet on it.

We can give you a couple of tips for avoiding the spotlight.

- Manage your drinking. We'll talk about alcohol next, but nursing your drinks, making yourself a mixed drink with very little alcohol in it, and keeping some food in your stomach are a few good party tricks.

- Take a nap. No, not at the party, the afternoon before the party. For some reason college parties are late night affairs. Most of the time you'll be heading out for the evening no earlier than 10:00. Why? We don't know, it just works that way. But mix alcohol and exhaustion and you get over-emotional. So take a nap!

- Use the buddy system to avoid beer goggling and relationship sabotage. No matter how responsible you think you are, ask a friend to keep an eye on you, so you don't leave the party with some girl or guy, especially if you or they are in a relationship with someone else, or if it's a connection that wouldn't happen if you were sober. Make a vow that you are leaving the party with your friend!

- Put your friends and roommate first in questionable hook-up situations. You may think you really want to get together with someone, but if it's going to ruin your living situation or a good friendship it's not worth it.

"The typical student is friendly, hard-working, and beer-loving. Although there are other options, parties (and alcohol in general) dominate the social scene."

—James Madison University Student

It's Your Party

While we're talking about parties, we should talk about hosting them. If the following advice makes it sound like we're uptight, that's too bad. Like every annoying person who gives advice, we're telling you that you'll thank us for it later. Before you throw a party in your room, think about the consequences. You, not anyone else, are the one who's going to get into trouble if anything goes wrong. So if your neighbor complains about the noise, your R.A. catches your underage guests (or you) in the hall with a drink, or someone ends up throwing up in the bathroom, or worse, in the infirmary because they had way too much to drink, it's your butt that's on the line. It's also your room that things are getting spilled in and your stuff that's likely to get broken. Still, it can be great to get all of your friends together, and hey, somebody has to throw the parties. So if you think you can handle it, here are a few suggestions to pull it off smoothly:

- If your R.A. is a reasonable type, let him know that you're having a party. Don't say, "I'm buying a few cases and having some friends over." If your R.A. knows that you're underage, he can't knowingly let you drink. However, if he expects some noise and people, he'll be less likely to come to your room and find out exactly what's going on. If you were courteous enough to fill him in, he may cut you a break and call you to tell you to turn it down, before coming to your room in person.

- Invite your neighbors. What better way to avoid complaints than to have all of your neighbors at the party. Don't forget the people who live above and below you.

- Buy some munchies, and provide some non-alcoholic beverages. You're doing yourself a favor if you prevent your guests from drinking on an empty stomach. And you're doing your guests a favor if you don't assume that everyone drinks.

- If people are driving to your party, take their keys and make sure there's a designated driver. Make it clear that people are welcome to stay on your couch, your floor, etcetera.

- Don't drink too much. You need to stay on top of things. If anything goes wrong you need to be able to make decisions and maybe talk to fun people like your R.A. or campus security.

If You Don't Drink

Our discussion thus far has been based in large part on the idea that drinking is an integral element of parties. For better or for worse, this is often true. Social drinking is part of the American psyche, from cocktail parties to beer at football games to champagne receptions, and college tends to take this mentality to the extreme. That doesn't mean that you will have no social life if you don't want to drink. But you will find that these years are just the beginning of having to work a little harder to go down the less-traveled social road. If you don't feel comfortable being around people who do drink, it may limit your party options in college. You may have to look around a bit, but you will find other people who share your views on alcohol, and you can create your own social scene with them. You can also go to plays, go to the movies, go out to eat, and do any number of other things that are alcohol-free. It may seem like you can't have a life without drinking, but remember that you managed just fine without it up until now.

It is also entirely possible to hang out with and be friends with people who do drink. In fact, it can be pretty amusing to watch people act like complete drunken idiots when you're sober. Don't make a big deal out of the fact that you don't drink. If you do, people may feel like you're passing judgment on them because they do. Or you may make people feel self-conscious for having a drink, because you're not. Get yourself a soda as soon as you arrive at the party. As long as you have a cup in your hand, chances are people won't give a second thought to what's in it. However, don't be afraid to stand up for yourself if anyone gives you a hard time about not drinking. You have just as much of a right to say no as they do to say yes. If someone is jerk enough to pressure you, you probably don't want to hang out with them anyway. We'll talk a little more about this when we talk about alcohol.

ALCOHOL

It's Everywhere

"About 1 percent of the students do not drink. Maybe that's pushing it. Alcohol is everywhere."

—**University of the South Student**

For better or for worse, alcohol is everywhere on college campuses. Despite the increasing efforts of college administrations to educate students about the detrimental aspects of alcohol consumption, students can find whatever type of booze they're looking for at virtually any time.

We need to be realistic here. We both drank during our four years in college. In fact, we're not sure that all on-campus drinking is bad. We certainly had a lot of fun at parties and other functions where alcohol was served. As a result, rather than preaching about the virtues of alcohol prohibition, we're going to try and help you be aware of the college drinking scene and its downfalls.

In large part, the prevalence of alcohol on-campus is a product of the structure of college campuses. As everyone knows, the legal drinking age in all fifty states is twenty-one. Practically though, the drinking age acts only as an enforceable barrier on the purchase of alcohol, rather than it's consumption. On college campuses the drinking age is virtually unenforceable because students who are over twenty-one purchase the alcohol for the consumption of every member of the student body.

It seems that many colleges have resigned themselves to the fact that the residence life staffs and the campus security system can enforce the laws in only the most egregious cases of underage drinking. Even if colleges were to make the elimination of illegal on-campus drinking their number one policy goal, they couldn't possibly hire enough manpower or investigate every instance of drinking to have a significant impact on the problem. The reality is that most on-campus drinking goes on inside rooms and at parties where campus officials rarely are made aware of the problem. It would be impossible to have campus security sweep all the rooms in all the residence halls even on the smallest campus.

As a result of the difficulty in policing on-campus drinking, it has become prevalent and accepted. You're all adults now, though. Notwithstanding the legal drinking age, you have to make some choices for yourself. Not all of these choices are easy to make. However, you have to be strong in your convictions. If you do not want to drink, at any point in college or in the rest of your life, don't. Be proud of not drinking. We never ran into anyone in college who thought someone was a loser for not drinking. The peer pressure you'll get in college will be a lot more subtle than that. Stand up for yourself and simply tell people that drinking is not your thing.

If you do choose to drink, you need to understand all the responsibility that comes with making that decision. Not every person who drinks in college is an alcoholic, a misfit, or a slacker. In fact, we know a heck of a lot of people who are doing quite well and drank in college. The rest of this chapter strives to give everyone an overview of drinking in college. (There are also some good stories.) Since you have to make your own decisions, it's important that they be informed.

Don't Forget: If You're Under Twenty-One, It's Illegal

That's right, ladies and gentlemen, it's as illegal as any other crime. Different states have crafted different laws prohibiting and assigning penalties for underage drinking, but they all have them. This means that if you get caught drinking underage you can be subjected to monetary fines, jail time, community service, and alcohol rehabilitation programs. More importantly, you will have a criminal record because you are no longer a minor. Yeah, yeah, we know. You can be drafted, sent to war, and pay taxes, but you can't have a beer. We don't make the laws. If you don't like it write your State Assemblyman or Senator.

It's not only the local police that you'll have to contend with if you decide to drink under age. You'll also be under the domain of campus security. It's true that when Joe was an improvisational comedian he made a lot of fun of campus security people. After all, they do have a predisposition for eating donuts and attempting to police the campus with a starter pistol. Nonetheless, as a student you've undoubtedly been given a code of student conduct that lists a number of school-promulgated rules and regulations that you have to follow. In this code, we're sure you'll find a section on drinking that basically says that your college can take any and all action they deem appropriate if you are found to have violated the school's alcohol policy. The school probably promises everything from a slap on the wrist to expulsion for those who violate its rules.

Our advice is to take the school's alcohol policy seriously. When we discussed cheating on exams we said that the school would make an example of a student caught cheating in order to send a message to the rest of the miscreant members of the student body. The same thing holds true for violations of the alcohol policy. Your college will be looking to hang you from the gallows in order to send the message that they're serious about alcohol restriction on campus. As we said before, schools are already frustrated by their relative ineffectiveness in curbing on-campus drinking. Don't let yourself become the school's example of what happens to those students who drink on campus.

Just keep in mind that there's a lot to lose if you get caught drinking underage. You do not want to ever feel obligated to explain away why you were brought up on criminal charges, n'est-ce pas? The easy way for you to avoid this ever becoming a problem is to never do anything that would increase your chance of getting caught. Theoretically, you could get caught just for drinking a beer in your room. However, this rarely happens. Practically, people get caught for underage drinking because they're belligerent to authority, drunk and disorderly, and creating a public nuisance. All of this leads toward what we've said before: Drink responsibly and know your limits.

Drinking Responsibly

It seems clear that the most accepted alcohol on campus is the old standby: beer. Beer is the alcohol of choice because it's cheap and easy to get. We don't remember anyone throwing parties with cases of Heineken and Anchor Steam. Instead, it was the Meister Brau, Glacier Bay, Piels, and Schlitz that often appeared. This is because you can get a case of these, depending on where you live, for about ten bucks.

Moreover, beer is easy to purchase. In many states you can buy beer at grocery stores and delicatessens. This translates into an increased availability and a lesser inspection for both legal and underage individuals trying to purchase beer. Put simply, if you're nineteen and trying to buy a case of beer, you're a lot more likely to succeed than if you walked up to the counter looking to purchase two bottles of Jack Daniel's.

Now, we're not going to shoot down beer. We like beer, and we liked beer when we were in college too. There are some things you need to know though. Beer is alcohol. This seems like a simple enough proposition, but the corollaries are important. You can get drunk on beer just as easily and just as quickly as any other type of alcohol. Similarly, this means that you can get just as addicted to beer as any other alcohol, and that it does as much damage to your system. We've seen a bunch of people get alcohol poisoning from beer. We've also seen people pass out, throw up on themselves, and choke on their own vomit. That would be a nice post card home, right? If you're going to drink beer, take it as seriously as drinking any other type of booze.

Just ask our friend Chris. Chris decided it would be kind of fun to see how many beers he could "shot gun." To do this, Chris basically figured out a way to make full cans of beer slide down his throat with the force of gravity. (No, we're not going to tell you how to do it.) Chris figured out that he could shot gun a beer in about five seconds. With this new bit of knowledge, he downed a six pack in a matter of minutes. Oh, yeah, we forgot to mention that Chris weighed about 170 pounds (fully dressed and soaking wet). Feeling pretty good, Chris went to the campus dining hall and sat next to the woman he had been trying to meet for weeks. Chris didn't seem to notice that she was sitting with an older couple. Well, to make a long story short, Chris found out that a chicken dinner doesn't go to well with a shotgunned six pack. He blew chunks everywhere, all over the woman and the older couple. (Stinks to be in the line of fire, right?) Needless to say, the woman was mortified and wouldn't go within miles of Chris. Slightly more upset though, was the couple that Chris was also sitting with: the Dean and his wife, who had come to experience the dining hall and meet some of the students. We think that Chris is still filing papers and mowing the Dean's lawn. We've changed the names here, but you get the point.

There is also plenty of other alcohol on campus. Whisky, tequila, gin, vodka, and the rest are all available. These aren't as easy to purchase if you're underage, but rest assured that some twenty-one-year-olds will be willing to buy these for anyone wanting them. Every year in the fall a bunch of freshmen end up in the hospital because they didn't think that a tall glass of vodka seemed like too much. After all, you wouldn't hesitate to drink a tall glass of orange juice, right? These students have a tough bit of explaining to do to their parents and the administration.

So-called "hard alcohol" is dangerous because of the quickness and strength with which it affects the consumer. The typical situation goes like this: A person has one shot with a beer chaser. He doesn't feel anything a couple of minutes later, so he has another. A couple of minutes later still nothing. Frustrated, he has a third and fourth shot with beer chasers. Now that a half-hour has gone by, he begins to feel a little lightheaded, but he figures he's having fun. He's begun to lose his guarded enthusiasm. So, saying "what the hell," he has a fifth shot forty-five minutes after the first. Boom, lights out. The room's spinning, his speech is slurred, he feels nauseated. He knows he's in trouble, but it's too late. The alcohol has gone into his bloodstream and even vomiting now won't save him. And so, one hour after he had his first shot, he's passed out on the floor of the bathroom, dry heaving because everything in his stomach is gone. His friends panic and call health services. The scene concludes with the student hooked up to an IV in the hospital, parents having driven or flown into town to see him.

That's the typical scene. The other thing that sometimes happens is that the friends are too scared of getting busted to call health services and they take the drunk person home and put them to bed. Unfortunately, that person never wakes up. If you think it doesn't happen, you're wrong.

Then there are the mixed drinks. People make mixed drinks in college for a lot of reasons: There are a lot of calories in beer; you can get drunk quicker on a mixed drink than on beer; and they taste good. The key here is that you understand that just because you are masking the taste of the alcohol in the drink doesn't mean that it's not there. In fact, it may be that mixed drinks are more dangerous than straight shots, because people drink them quicker and have more of them because they can't taste the alcohol. (We suppose we should point out that when we say mixed drinks, we don't mean gin and tonics, we mean the common college drinks, such as rum and cola, vodka and cranberry juice, vodka and orange juice, and similar concoctions.) Even if you find that it's easier to down a Sea Breeze than a shot of vodka, they've got the same alcohol content.

As a final note on mixed drinks, we beg you never to drink anything that you don't know the exact ingredients of. If you've been drinking "Blue stuff" all night, you're in trouble. Not only can these drinks be spiked with deadly things such as grain alcohol, they can be made with a variety of other drugs. You wouldn't eat food that you didn't know of, so don't drink unknown drinks.

Our friend, H., is a noted authority on this subject. (Sorry, H., the story had to be told.) We all went out to a bar in New York City one night, and H. began drinking Sea Breezes. After a couple, though, H., big flirt that she is, asked the bartender to make her anything he thought she'd like. Bad call. H. had Long Island Iced Teas, Melon Balls, Sex on the Beaches, Lemon Drops, and some other un-Godly drink called "The Red Thing." By the time we left, H. was three sheets to the wind. Walking home, we had to stop at every other corner so that Melanie could hold H.'s hair back while she chucked into people's plants, trash cans, and onto the street. This was not H.'s finest hour. Not only did she mix drinks, she didn't know what she was drinking. She's going to get sick just reading this again!

Some drunk stories don't end with people throwing up and worshipping the porcelain goddess. Some are worse and the person wishes they'd passed out before doing what they did! Take Melanie, for instance. She proved that turning twenty-one doesn't give you automatic immunity from making an idiot out of yourself. Joe's dearest was quite the actress in college. Once every year, the college dramatic society had a formal ball where those individuals involved in the theater, as well as the campus big wigs, gathered for a night of dancing and awards presentations. Well, Melanie had been drinking just a wee bit during the ball, and had gotten tipsy. Joe happened to be at the ball that year and happened to look up and see his friend, the President of the university, beckoning him over. Gee, guess who Joe found standing next to the President and the Dean of Students who was with him? That's right. Melanie, complete with drink in hand, discussing politics and making absolutely no sense as one syllable gently blended into another. The President gave Joe a big smile, slapped him on the back, politely introduced him to Melanie, and excused himself. The Governor is a good man and also a friend of Melanie's. He wouldn't even think of embarrassing her by mentioning their conversation ever again. Melanie, though, much to Joe's continuing amusement, is still absolutely mortified. (Joe insisted that this story go into the book just so it could live on infinitely.) The moral is that even if you're legally able to drink, have fun, and not hurt yourself or anyone else, you can still be sorry in the a.m.. Drink responsibly and know your limits.

There's one final point about responsible drinking we'd like to touch on. Friends don't let friends beer goggle. No, sorry, that's not it. We're serious here. *Do not drive drunk.* You've heard all this before so we'll make our comments short and to the point. Even if you don't care about wrapping yourself around a tree and leaving your parents devastated at the loss of their child, please think about the other person or people you're likely to hurt or kill by driving under the influence of alcohol. Don't be a selfish schmuck. If you're drinking, don't drive.

OTHER DRUGS

Marijuana

Without a doubt, the second most popular drug to alcohol on American campuses today is marijuana. It hasn't become the focus of the social scene as alcohol has, but it's pretty much everywhere.

We're not particularly interested in getting into a policy discussion over whether the use of marijuana is any more or less serious than the use of alcohol. As a matter of law this question is moot. Applicable laws universally say that possession and use of marijuana, with the very rare exception for specific medicinal purposes, is illegal. There are no other exceptions. It doesn't matter if you're twenty-one or eighteen, if you are using marijuana you are committing a criminal act.

Colleges do not overlook the criminal use of marijuana the way they may overlook minor violations of their alcohol policy. It's our experience that colleges have, as a matter of policy, decided to turn students that are found possessing or using marijuana over to the local police. By doing this, colleges can make sure that there is a consistency in their drug policy and that no one gets biased treatment.

We're not naive enough to think that we could stop you from using marijuana if you want to. However, just so you know, if you do get caught smoking pot, you're definitely getting expelled and you may be headed for jail.

Everything Else

If you're involved with drugs such as cocaine, amphetamines, and barbiturates, you need to get yourself quickly to a treatment center and a psychiatrist. All these drugs are available on campus to varying degrees, but just stay away from them. Forget getting caught, getting expelled or getting a criminal record. You're on a path toward killing yourself. We have only one thing to say on this topic: Stay away from people who use these drugs, and if you get involved yourself, seek treatment quickly.

Boy Meets Girl or Girl Meets Boy
(and All the Combinations Thereof)

Dating and thinking about dating are two of the primary activities on campus. A whole new population of people to meet, combined with the newfound freedom of living away from home, throws everyone into a veritable feeding frenzy. One of the coolest things about the dating scene at college is that you start with a clean slate. Remember how in high school there were always a handful of girls and guys who everyone wanted to go out with? Conversely, there were always a few people who were chubby or shy in sixth grade and never outgrew that image. Well, all the preconceptions are gone now. Not only do people not know what people thought of you in high school, but, more importantly, they don't care. You're free to meet new people, redefine your style, and develop great new relationships, and you will. We're not going to tell you how to get a date, first because we're sure you know how to do this, and second because there's no formula for that one! What we can tell you about are some of the things that may be new to the relationships you have in college, and the ways that you can best look out for number one (that's you).

Deep Thoughts . . . by Melanie and Joe

Know right now that college relationships can get pretty intense. You have the opportunity to spend almost twenty-four hours a day with your significant other. Any time that you're not in class—and sometimes you have the same classes—you can be together. This can be great for relationships, but it can also make you lose perspective. When you focus entirely on one person, any disagreement you have seems catastrophic, and any time of separation becomes traumatic. Obviously this isn't the healthiest state to put yourself in. Many people also make the mistake of neglecting all of their other friends, or of leaving their circle of friends for that of their boyfriend or girlfriend. Take it from us, you need to maintain your relationships with your friends. In other words, have a life outside your relationship.

During freshman year, a friend of Melanie's, we'll call her B., started dating a guy who was a junior. He was great, and his friends were great, and before long B. was spending all of her time with them. Melanie and her other friends weren't mad at B., but after a while they didn't think to ask her to join them in their plans. Why would they? She always had plans with her boyfriend and his group.

This was all fine until about six months later when B. and her boyfriend started fighting. His friends weren't bad people, but they had known him for three years and felt that they had to remain loyal to him, which made it hard for them to hang out with B. Suddenly B. was calling her old friends, the ones she hadn't had time for in a long time, and they understandably felt like they were obviously her second choice. Everyone ended up feeling bad. There is a happy ending; B. and her old friends eventually made peace.

However, all of this could have been avoided if B. had maintained a part of her life that was not dependent upon her relationship with her boyfriend. By the way, this advice is will apply far beyond your college years.

Smart Sex

We know that you've had sex education classes, probably since elementary school. People have been preaching to you about safe sex for a long time already. The truth is that a lot of students become sexually active in high school, so, regardless of your own experiences you probably know the score already. However, it's safe to say that sex will play a larger role in your life as you get older and progress through college and even graduate school. So if sex didn't factor into your life in high school, now is a good time to give some thought to how you want to handle your sex life and what your options are. What we're saying here is basic, so feel free to skip the parts you've already heard a million times.

Often, the smartest decision you can make about sex is not to have it. You're not going to get pregnant or get AIDS or any other STD if you're not having sex with anyone. That said, we realize that abstinence is far from the most popular choice in college. You're a grown-up now; you're involved in grown-up relationships. Sex can be a great part of a relationship when the timing is right and both of you know what you're doing. We talked before about how intense college relationships can be, and when you spend so much time with the person you're dating, you may start thinking about sex pretty quickly. Only you can decide when the time is right. Just remember that a good relationship will last as long as you need to wait.

One of the biggest obstacles to smart sex in college is undoubtedly alcohol. Many people have severe lapses of judgment when they've been drinking. You've heard the jokes about waking up with someone that you don't remember going to bed with. Well, it's not funny when it happens to you, and it can be dangerous. If you're drunk, not only may you have sex that you'll regret later, you are also more likely to have unprotected sex, which is definitely no laughing matter. Remember the buddy system we talked about at parties? It's always a good idea to have someone keeping track of you when you're drinking. Not only will your friend tell you to think twice before you leave with someone, he or she can also keep an eye out for anyone pressuring you to leave or do anything else. If you've been drinking, it's never a good idea to leave the party with someone that you don't know very well. Even if you don't think you're going to have sex, it's amazing how fast things happen when two drunk people are together. Even if all you do is pass out together, in the morning you face what's known as the Walk of Shame. In other words, you have to make your way back to your room in what are obviously the clothes you had on the night before. People who don't know you aren't going to believe that nothing happened. Maybe you don't care what people say, but know that they'll be saying it.

A relaxed attitude toward safe sex can also be a problem on college campuses. It's easy to delude yourself into believing that it's not risky to have unprotected sex with one of your nice, clean-cut classmates. Don't bet on it, even if you're monogamous. You are the only person whose fidelity you can truly vouch for, and even a faithful partner may transmit a virus to you that he didn't know he had. Melanie counseled more than one resident who got an STD or was freaking out because he thought that his girlfriend was pregnant. Think about it, is one sexual encounter worth the possible consequences? Is it worth getting AIDS and dying? Using a condom is so simple that there's no excuse for having sex without one. The campus health services office often dispenses contraceptives; many give out condoms for free. Women can schedule gynecological exams here, and get prescriptions for contraceptives. And women, if you are sexually active, it's important that you do get regular exams. Not all STDs and infections cause symptoms, and if you don't get regular check-ups you're risking permanent damage to your reproductive system. Remember that some of the more popular methods of birth control, such as the pill, the diaphragm, and sponges, may be effective protection against pregnancy but they don't protect you against STDs. The charges for medical services in campus infirmaries vary. If, for some reason, you can't afford the help you need at school, ask the health center to refer you to a free or low-cost clinic such as those offered by the state or Planned Parenthood.

No Means No

This is a total bummer of a topic, but one that we have to discuss. Unfortunately, rape, and in particular date rape, is a reality on college campuses. In chapter 8, we'll talk more about campus safety and avoiding assault, but here we'll talk about date rape. It could be because dorm living makes ending up alone in a bedroom a lot easier, because people act irrationally when they're drunk, or because many people are dealing with their first sexual encounters. Whatever the reasons, date rape happens all too often on campus. We'd like to start by saying that, without exception, no means no. It doesn't matter how drunk a woman is, or if she goes to a man's room with him after a party, if she says no, that's as far as it goes. If you're getting mixed signals about what your partner wants, take that as a no. In fact, the only truly safe thing to do is to wait until you get a clear yes. Remember, there are two sides to every coin, so your actions may later be interpreted in a way that you never intended.

There are a number of factors that can add up to a potential date rape situation. Once again, alcohol is often involved. Here are some tips for staying in control and staying safe:

- **Know your limits.** We've talked about this before: Be careful about the amount you drink.

- **Think twice before you leave a party with someone, especially if you've been drinking.** This is another good time to use the buddy system. Make a pact to leave the party with the friend that you came with. And if you really want to do differently, at least let your friend know who you're leaving with and where you're going. It's always a good idea to let someone know where you are.

- **Remember that you *always* have the right to say no.** It doesn't matter if you go to your partner's room, if you've been making out for two hours, or even if you've had sex with this partner before. If you don't want to go any further, *you always have the right to say no.*

- **Be vocal about what you want and don't want.** Sometimes you may feel that your actions are communicating your desires, but what's clear to you may not be getting across to your partner. If you want him to stop, say "stop." If no is what you mean, come right out and say it. If you're make yourself clear at every step along the way, it makes it more difficult for things to get out of control.

- **If you feel uncomfortable in any situation, leave.** Trust your instincts. If you feel uncomfortable or pressured in any situation, leave right away. Don't feel embarrassed or worry about hurting the other person's feelings; taking care of yourself is what's important in this situation.

- **Make a scene.** If you ever feel trapped or scared, make a scene. Run or start screaming. Chances are that whoever the person is who has put you in that situation will back off when they think help is on the way.

Hopefully, you will never find yourself the victim of a date rape. If you do, there are a couple of things you should remember:

- **You are not to blame.** Many women feel that they must have caused what has happened to them. They often think, "It happened because I was drunk," "I should have fought back harder," or "Maybe I didn't say no clearly enough." If you had sex that you didn't want, you are a victim. Don't feel guilty.

- **Make sure you are safe.** Call 911, campus security, or at least one of your friends. You need to be somewhere where you feel safe and have someone with you after such a traumatic incident, to give you support and help you get help.

- **You should consider reporting the rape to the authorities.** Deciding to report a rape is a very personal and very difficult decision. Remember though, that reporting the incident doesn't mean you are committing yourself to pressing charges. What it does mean is that evidence will be collected, without which you would have no evidence if you decide later that you do want to press charges. By no means should you feel obligated to be a hero, but if you do press charges you may prevent the same thing from happening to someone else.

- **Take care of yourself.** Rape is not something that you get over in a few days. Definitely see a doctor. Make sure that you weren't physically injured and think about getting tested for STDs and AIDS. You can also ask your doctor for referrals to a psychologist, counselor, or support group that can help you deal with the emotional repercussions of what has happened to you.

GET INVOLVED

"What?" you ask. "What do you mean by 'get involved'? When will I have time with all of these classes, papers, exams, and parties?" Although it sounds like you will be busy (and you often will be), you will have time to get involved in other activities on campus. As important as your academics are, you are only physically in class for a few hours a day. Even if your goal is straight As every semester, you can't and won't spend every minute that you're not in class studying and working. You'd be in the loony bin in at matter of weeks. Plus, if you're only worrying about your grades, you're not seeing the big picture.

Think of it this way: Everyone who goes to college ends up with a transcript full of grades. There's nothing special about that. In fact, even having a transcript full of *good* grades won't always differentiate you from other students. You know what a graduate school or employer is going to think about you if all you did in college was get good grades. Well, we'll tell you: They're going to think you're a one-dimensional person who wouldn't know how to get a life if it bit you on the butt. Why should they admit or hire a person who had great grades, if they can get someone who had great grades, played varsity football, is a gourmet cook, and volunteers at the local nursing home? Okay, so that example is a little extreme, but you get the idea. The things that you do outside class can tell people important things about who you are as a person, like whether you can be a team player, if you care about other people, and if you're motivated to pursue other interests. So get involved. You can have a lot of fun and round out your resume at the same time.

> *"One of the highlights of my college life is being involved in some of the various clubs. We have a lot of fun together, and it makes the stress more bearable."*
>
> **—Whittier College Student**

Still not convinced? How about the fact that getting involved in other activities is a bona fide excuse for closing the books sometimes? Or that campus organizations and activities are a way to meet people who share your interests? And joining a group may give you the opportunity to meet that special someone that you keep seeing around campus. If the guy or girl that you've been lusting after in your Bio class is a member of the ski team, you could be cozied up on the chair lift next weekend.

> *"Getting involved in clubs and organizations helps me keep my sanity."*
>
> **—Wittenberg University Student**

Now that we've got you pumped up to join every club on campus, we also have to tell you not to go overboard. You don't want to get involved in too many extracurricular activities at the expense of your academics. You do want to be a real contributor in the clubs and activities that you get involved in, which means you should only get involved in as many as you have time to do well in. If you send in a resume that says you played basketball, played in the band, were the student body Treasurer, wrote for the newspaper, and were a member of the French, Drama, and Glee clubs, people are going to wonder how much you could actually have contributed by spreading yourself so thin (that's if they don't think you're flat-out lying). You have four years to try new things. Better to start with one or two and add activities as you figure out how much time and energy you have. Some people thrive on being super busy. Melanie always found that having a lot to do forced her to get organized and resulted in her accomplishing more than when she had a lot of free time. Having a packed schedule certainly doesn't give you room to procrastinate. You may find this works for you, or you may find that you need more downtime to keep your energy level up. Add one new activity at a time until you strike the right balance.

"There are more activities, guest speakers, and seminars available than I can attend. The school and campus life are what you make of them."

—Southern Methodist University Student

So Many Options, So Little Time

Now you have to figure out what you want to do. Think about what you did in high school. Were you involved in student government? Did you sing in the choir? Were you a star athlete? Maybe you'd like to continue some of these activities in college. With your past experience you probably have expertise and good ideas that you can share with a new group. You should also think about what you're interested in. From journalism to modern dance, you'll probably be able to find some campus organization that fits the bill. Extracurricular activities are a great way to explore new interests, because you'll meet people who share your enthusiasm, and you won't get graded on your performance. Who knows, you may try writing for the school paper and discover a talent that you want to develop into a career. Don't be afraid to try new things. Going back to the resume-enhancing angle, it always looks good to have a well-rounded list of interests. You can probably find descriptions of all of the campus clubs, teams, organizations, and activities in your student handbook, and many of them you'll see recruiting participants on campus. But just to give you an idea of what your options may be we came up with a list:

- Fraternities and Sororities—We'll talk in detail about these later in the chapter.
- Sports teams—Ditto
- Singing groups—Choirs, a capella groups, etcetera.
- Band or Orchestra

- Drama Club—Not just for actors. In addition to auditioning for a role in a production, you can try your hand at costume or set design, work as a house manager, work in the lighting booth, and more.

- Student Government—Have complaints or ideas about life on campus? Do something about it: Run for election or help the candidate of your choice get elected.

- Newspaper—Give journalism a try by writing for the school paper. You could write editorials, cover sporting events, review campus productions or the movies at the local theater. The options are endless. If you want to pursue writing as a career, now's the time to get started.

- Campus Radio Stations—Several of our friends had a blast as DJs for the college radio station. Where else will you have a chance to play good music and dedicate songs to whoever you want?

- Language Clubs—French, Spanish, German, Japanese, Russian, Sanskrit—You name the language and there's probably a club where you can practice speaking, organize screenings of foreign films, and sponsor speakers and other cultural activities for the campus.

- Academic Clubs—In addition to language clubs, almost every academic department has clubs or sponsors activities for interested students.

- Campus Tour Guides—Love your school? Let prospective students know, as you give them a tour and answer their questions.

- Volunteer Opportunities—There are lots of organizations that would love to put your extra time to good use. Whether you work at a soup kitchen, the legal aid society, or the humane society, you'll find the time you spend there very rewarding.

As you can see, there are a lot of choices on our list, and we're sure there are probably many more that we didn't cover. The best part of the wide selection is that you can shop around. Try going to a couple of meetings or events before you officially join any group, because even though you may like the idea of some groups, you may find that you don't hit it off with the other members or that the format of the meetings bores you to tears. You don't want to make any snap decisions, because what you're talking about is making a time commitment, and your time is valuable. There are certain activities and groups that will require much more of your time (and energy) than others, depending on how involved you become. Now is a good time to fill you in on two of these.

Greek Life

What Is a Fraternity/Sorority?
Delta Phi is a fraternity. Sorry, we figured we'd get that plug for Joe's fraternity in right off the bat so that you know where we stand on this issue. Literally, a fraternity is a "group of brothers" and a sorority is a "group of sisters." In practice, both are very close groups of male or female friends who have chosen to publicly associate themselves as such.

When you first arrive on campus you will undoubtedly become aware of the Greek system if your school has one. You'll see houses with strange letters you don't know how to pronounce and upperclass students walking around with matching sweatshirts. The way most people get their first glimpse of the Greek system is by attending a party thrown by a fraternity or sorority. Don't be put off by the image you might have from watching *Animal House* too many times. Go and check it out.

The Greek system at each school develops a formal process of having new students get involved with fraternities and sororities; it's called "rush." There are both national and local fraternities and sororities, and this is your chance to meet them. Rush is basically your opportunity to go to each of the fraternity or sorority houses and meet the members. Some schools structure it so that you have to register for rush. After registering, these schools require you to go to each house at least once so that you give everyone a fair shot of meeting you and yourself of meeting them. Other schools only assign the dates of rush and leave all the events up to the individual houses to schedule. At these schools, you'll see fliers and schedules of upcoming events at each house. For example, Wednesday night during Delta Phi rush might be "Boys Night Out," and you'll have a night out on the town hanging out with the brothers. Rush is a good thing. There is absolutely no obligation to join any fraternity or sorority during rush. Instead, you can take your time figuring out if you're interested in joining the Greek system, going to as few or as many events as you'd like, and finding out why so many people for so many years have seen the Greek system as worthwhile.

"Rush is a major part of life at school. Whether you're a freshman or an upperclassman, the Greeks are the ones hosting the weekend entertainment."

—Southern Methodist University Student

After rush has ended, the Greek system will ask you whether or not you intend to get involved. In fact, they'll probably ask for your decision by a certain date. If you decide that the Greek system isn't for you, you simply walk away. We'll be honest about this. It's true that sometimes fraternities and sororities are anxious to get good members and are disappointed when students decide not to participate in the Greek system. However, we don't know of anyone who was ever harassed for his decision to walk away.

If you do decide to participate, you will be asked to commit to one fraternity or sorority. By this time though, it's likely that you'll have a good idea of which house you feel most comfortable at and with which men and women you'd like to associate. There is one catch. You have to be asked to participate by the house you commit to. Most schools refer to a particular house asking you to commit as a "bid." If you accept the bid, then you've committed to continue the process with that specific house. If you decline your bid, you're free to accept any other bid you receive or to not participate in the Greek system at all. It's a popular misconception about fraternities and sororities that membership is not entirely voluntary. That's simply not true. Even when you accept a bid indicating that you've chosen a specific house to get involved with within the Greek system, *you can leave at any time.*

Once you commit to a specific house, that fraternity's or sorority's system essentially takes over. There is usually a celebration welcoming in all the students who have decided to try and become members of the house. These individuals as a group are usually referred to as "pledges." At this time, your fraternity or sorority will explain to you what the process is to become a member. The processes are so different from house to house that we won't try to give you examples. However, it's a safe bet that the brothers or sisters in the house will expect the pledges to show that they care about the house, its members, and its overall success.

After a specified amount of time, usually a semester or a year, the pledges become members of the fraternity or sorority. Is it that easy? No, of course not. Nothing worthwhile in life is that easy, and if it was, there wouldn't be anything special about "being Greek."

We suppose that it's important to speak about "hazing" here. "Hazing" is physical or emotional abuse by the members of the house toward the pledges. All national fraternities and sororities have pledged not to allow hazing. It's entirely inappropriate and it shouldn't happen to you. We can't tell you that no hazing ever occurs any more. We'd be lying. We can say, though, that in becoming a brother in his fraternity, Joe never had to go through anything that made him uncomfortable. Remember, if you feel uncomfortable you can and should leave.

On a more positive note, becoming a member of the Greek system has its rewards. First, you'll have a group of friends for life. For example, Joe's best man, George Eliou, was a Delta Phi Brother, and another member of our wedding party, Pete Bonovota, was Joe's fraternity Big Brother. Also, you'll always have something to do. There are parties, sporting events, Greek Week, Spring Break, and other Greek functions to attend. Finally, you'll meet tons of people. This may help you later when you're searching for a job or looking to get into graduate school.

That's the structure of the Greek system in a nutshell. We could be more specific, but the Greek systems at many schools are different. Check out rush at your school to get the full scoop.

Getting the Facts Straight

We figured we'd write this section for all of you who skipped the above because you've made up your mind about the Greek system. We'd like a chance to give you our perspective. At the outset, it's important to understand that the Greek system isn't for everybody.

Hey, if you're not interested in becoming Greek, that's cool. Just make sure that you're basing your decision on the facts:

- **Don't rely on the stereotypes to make your decision.** Did you think we'd never talk to you about this? We've been honest with you up to this point in the book, we'll continue to do so. Fraternities and sororities have a mixed history. Not all of the scenes in *Animal House* are false. Seriously though, it's true that every year there are students involved in the Greek system who are killed because of alcohol consumption, hurt because of hazing, and get in trouble for breaking or disregarding the law. However, these incidents make most of the Greek system cringe with embarrassment and disgrace. We don't condone behavior that could potentially injure another person. However, these incidents are not the nationwide norm, and should not stand as the image of the Greek system. The only true way to get an accurate picture of the Greek system is to participate at your school and get involved with a specific chapter. Don't let the stereotypes dissuade you from getting your own, first-hand information.

"Although fraternity/sorority life is popular, it is not over-emphasized for those who do not participate."

—University of the South Student

"Life is ruled by the Greek system. All parties are Greek-related but are open to anyone; and most fraternities accept others."

—Sewanee University Student

- **Fraternities and sororities aren't weird cults.** They are made up of students just like you who have decided that they're interested in joining an on-campus group. To be sure, the level of commitment and interest in the group is higher than those of many other college clubs. However, the rewards that come with being a member of the Greek system are equally great.

- **The Greek system is not solely about drinking**. At it's core, the Greek system is about friendship. This certainly includes socializing, which on college campuses, as we've already discussed, includes alcohol. A fraternity or sorority isn't any more about drinking than any other group of friends is.

- **Members of the Greek system aren't all miscreants and intellectual zeros**. We've got news for you: look around and you'll see members of sororities and fraternities at every level of our society. The Greek system has been around a long, long time. For example, Joe's fraternity, Delta Phi, was founded at Union College in 1827 and his chapter, Gamma, began at NYU in 1841. Joe has brothers who are public relations men, emergency medical technicians, judges, businessmen, lawyers, members of the United Nations peacekeeping force, teachers, and commissioned officers in the United States Marine Corps. You pick a profession and you'll find several of its leaders are Greek.

- **Greeks don't hate non-Greeks**. This one is always a kicker. Some people feel that if you're not Greek then members of the fraternity and sorority systems don't want to have anything to do with you. This simply isn't true. Almost all fraternity social events are done open house, so that members of the college community can also participate. Moreover, you'll find Greeks involved in varsity sports, campus theater, blood drives, community cleanup projects, late night student security services, fund-raising, and lots of other college-wide projects. The fact is that many of the people who feel that Greeks are exclusionary haven't taken the time to research the Greek system or to try and get involved. Instead, they work on outmoded and misguided stereotypes that all true Greeks try to combat.

Okay, we suppose those are the biggies. You'll have to excuse us for rushing to the defense of the Greek system, but since it's been blamed for everything from the proliferation of nuclear arms to osteoporosis we thought it was time someone gave it a fair shake. Whether or not you decide to participate in the Greek system, you should make up your own mind on its benefits and drawbacks. Of course, as with everything else in college, don't be afraid to be yourself!

The Sporting Life

Varsity Sports

Are you the next Christian Laettner, Ki-Jana Carter, or Rebecca Lobo? Even if you're not, you may want to participate in varsity sports at your school.

Schools are placed into divisions based primarily on the size of their student bodies. For example, the schools you're likely to see playing sports on television, such as Penn State University, Notre Dame, Georgetown University, and Florida State University, are Division I schools. This means a number of things in terms of the amount of time and effort you'll have to put in to compete.

Student-athletes at Division I schools devote virtually all their time outside of class to their sport. Moreover, it's not easy to make the team at this level. You'll be competing with individuals who have devoted their whole lives to their sport and are naturally gifted athletes. You'll also be competing with the best for the sports scholarship money. Realistically, most students don't play at this level. If you are a golfer who shoots about ninety a round, you won't be teeing up with Tiger Woods at Stanford any time soon.

There are also Division II and III schools. The level of competition at these schools is still very high. However, many more students may have the opportunity to play at these schools. Keep in mind though, that even at this level students give up a considerable amount of time to their sport.

As a student-athlete, you will choose to add the pressure of a rigorous practice and game schedule to an already hectic college career. Nonetheless, you will still be expected to meet the same academic requirements that all students at your school must meet. Moreover, there are National Collegiate Athletic Association (NCAA) requirements that student-athletes at all levels must meet. Don't expect that you will get any special treatment because you're an athlete. In fact, many professors and students may be looking for you to make a mistake because they've accepted the stereotype of the college athlete who tries to slide by the system.

In short, it takes an especially dedicated person to compete as a student athlete at any level. Make sure you understand the pressures and demands of such a college career before you get involved.

Intramural Sports

For most students, intramurals offer a great way to stay active in sports without the demands of a varsity athletics program. In fact, since varsity athletes are banned from participating in intramural sports, you'll be competing against students just like yourself.

One great thing about intramurals is that there are typically tons of them. Basketball, baseball, football, hockey, volleyball, skiing, golf, and squash were all available at NYU. What's more, since they are intramurals, if you're into a sport that doesn't have a league, just create it! If you register your sport with the school, and you can show them that there are a number of students who would be interested in competing, they'll be happy to help. Who knows, you might discover that everyone on campus has been sitting around waiting for someone to take the initiative to create a croquet league.

For the record, don't kid yourself into believing that the level of competition at the intramural level isn't fierce. It is. Many intramural athletes may be able to play at a varsity level, but have chosen academics as their focus, or may have injuries and other such problems that prevented them from playing varsity sports. You won't notice that they're actually not varsity athletes when you're playing against them though. Just ask anyone who's ever played intramural football against Joe's friend Pete Bonovota. Pete was a guard for the New Jersey Division I football champions his senior year in high school. People didn't seem to notice that he was focused on his pre-med studies as they found themselves buried in the turf from one of Pete's blocks. You'll find similar people playing intramural sports at your school.

Intramurals are a great way to meet people, get some exercise, release some stress, and have some fun at school. If you love sports but aren't interested in playing varsity, get involved in intramurals.

No Excuses

After all of the brilliant and informed suggestions we've given you in this chapter, we can't imagine that you don't see some extra-curricular activities in your near future. Honestly, with all college campuses have to offer, you almost have to work harder to do nothing than you do to get involved. Even if you don't want to take on too many ongoing time commitments, there will be plenty of concerts, lectures, plays, sports events, and other happenings that you should take advantage of. So don't make excuses, make plans.

CHAPTER 8

Get A Job

WORKING WHILE YOU'RE IN SCHOOL

With the price of college these days, it's amazing that anyone gets to go at all. One thing most people have to do in order to scrape by financially in college is get a job. Luckily, college students generally don't have a problem finding jobs (unless they're looking to make the salary of a neurosurgeon).

There are a number of ways to cope with having a job while you're in school. Students take jobs on campus, part-time jobs off campus, weekend jobs and night jobs. There's no question that all of these options make life a little more complicated. Even though you'd think that the professors and administration would be sympathetic with your time commitments at work, they usually just expect you to have super-human time management skills. And you will have to keep yourself organized and work hard to use every hour effectively. Most importantly, though, you'll have to find a job that fits your lifestyle and lets you succeed at work and in school. After all, earning the money for your books won't do you any good if you never have time to open one. The rest of this chapter is designed to help you maintain both financial stability *and* your sanity.

Getting Started

Before you take on any job while you're in school, figure out how much time you can realistically spare. Get into the groove of your classes, see how heavy your workload is, and *then* look for work. Studying on the job, or spending your study time doing work for your job, does not qualify as handling things well. You owe it to yourself and your employer not to spread yourself too thin. You'll probably find that ten to twenty hours is as much as you can handle.

One of the best things you have going for you as a college student looking for a job is the campus career placement office. There you'll find people whose full-time job is to help you find one. You can start by having them work over your resume with you. You may not have much experience to list, but the career counselors can help you make what you do have sound ten times better. Six months as a salesperson at the Gap becomes retail sales experience in which you fielded customer inquiries and acted as a corporate representative to the public. That may be stretching things, but they can help you jazz up your experience. The career office is also the place to learn to write cover letters with flair and to practice your interview skills. You may even be able to schedule a mock interview that the career placement staff can use to critique you and give you advice. All of these skills will serve you well for the rest of your working years. Getting to know the staff at the center is another bonus, because they can be a lifeline when you near graduation and are looking for a permanent position.

If you want to get a job on campus, the career center is a one-stop source. You can usually find listings of everything that's available and put in applications right there. This is also the place to find "work-study" jobs. These are jobs that are given as part of your financial aid package, and, since you've proven that you need the money you earn to pay your tuition or pay for your books (not to subsidize your wardrobe), the hourly wages are higher than those of similar non-work-study positions.

Most career centers also post job openings around the community. Businesses in many college towns employ students and recruit through the career centers. Families looking for baby-sitters, elderly people looking for help with housework, and other people in the community may also contact the career office.

There are other avenues you should explore in addition to the Career Placement Office:

- Tell everyone you know that you're looking for a job. This includes other students, family who live in the area, friends of family who live in the area, and anyone you can think of. This is called networking, and it's a skill you'll use throughout your life. Many, many jobs are never advertised, because as soon as they open up, someone thinks of a friend or acquaintance who can fill the position. You want to be that person.

- Take a look through the classified section of the local paper.

- Stroll through town and look for Help Wanted signs.

- Call the places where you'd like to work. Maybe one of them has a position that's not being advertised. Even if they don't, they may like your initiative and keep you in mind for future positions. Find out who you can send a resume to, so you don't have to send a "To Whom it May Concern" letter.

These tips should put you well on your way toward gainful employment.

Campus Jobs

As a freshman, working on campus is a good idea. Your boss at a campus job is much more likely to be understanding when you need to adjust your hours to write a big paper or study for finals. First of all, they're used to student schedules. And since all of the other employees are probably students too, and all of you have crazy schedules the week before finals, you can usually find someone who wants to trade hours with you. The drawback of campus jobs is that they usually pay less, not usually much more than minimum wage, unless you have a work-study job. But the flexibility may make the lower pay worthwhile. Sometimes there are other bonuses that add to the compensation. Melanie worked in the school bookstore her freshman year and got a discount on everything she bought, including her textbooks. If you work in the registrar's office, you may be able to wrangle your way into all of the classes you want.

Typical campus jobs include:

- **Library Aid.** Put to use all of the library skills you've developed over the years. You may spend time reshelving and checking out books, helping out at the research desk, or working at the reserve or microfilm desk.

- **Food Services.** Busing tables and restocking the salad bar may not be glamorous tasks, but the hours are probably reasonable. Many campus food services also do catering for on-campus events, and you could work preparing or delivering food or acting as a server.

- **Research Assistant.** Professors are often working on articles or research projects and need someone to do the grunt work of digging up information, photocopying, and making phone calls. Developing a relationship with a professor, especially in your major department, is a great way to find a mentor, and as you do more work you may be entrusted with greater responsibility—eventually even helping with the writing. The professor will also be a great person to ask for a recommendation if you decide to apply to graduate school.

- **Residence Life Staff.** We talked about being a Resident Assistant in chapter 2. This job can have great rewards, including paying for part or all of your room and board expenses and looking good on your resume. However, the competition for these jobs is usually stiff, and it is a big time commitment.

- **Office Worker.** There are many offices on every campus: financial aid, bursar's, registrar's, alumni relations, admissions, various department offices, and more. Many of them need someone to act as a receptionist, answer phones, or do paperwork and filing.

- **Bookstore.** As we said above, the bookstore can be a great place to work if you get a discount. Since *everyone* comes into the store for something, it's also a very social place to work. You could work as a cashier, order textbooks, process invoices, stock the shelves, or all of the above.

- **Tutoring.** If you have expertise in a subject, tutoring may be the job for you. You probably have to get approval from the head of the academic department you want to work in.

- **Lab Assistant.** From Biology labs to French labs, students are needed to monitor other students, answer questions, and keep track of equipment. Again, you may need a professor's approval to get these jobs.

There are probably a lot of other jobs that we haven't thought of, but this should give you an idea of what you'll find on campus.

Off-Campus Jobs

You may be able to find a job off-campus that allows you flexible hours, but probably not to the same degree you'll find on campus. Don't expect too much understanding from your boss. When you accept the job, you're agreeing to be a responsible employee. So unless you talk to your supervisor ahead of time about decreasing your hours the week before finals, don't expect her to make special allowances for you. However, you may be able to find an off-campus job that pays more than the jobs at school. And you may find you like spending some time each week outside your normal boundaries.

Here are a few not-so-obvious things to look at when you're searching for an off-campus job:

- **Completely un-corporate jobs like baby-sitting or doing yard work.** They may not sound impressive, but you can find unusual hours to suit your schedule, and it can be nice to get to know a family in town.

- **Getting your foot in the door.** It's a good idea to start garnering experience in the field you think you might choose as your career. Remember that the job you're going to get is going to be super-entry level. But everyone pays their dues, and if you pay yours early, you may be on to bigger and better things even before you graduate.

- **Work can be play (or at least kind of).** If you are good at sports, see if a local gym or YMCA needs help. Maybe you can assist with the activities at an after-school program for kids, or assist one of the exercise class instructors. Who knows, even if you work as a desk clerk, maybe you can get use of the facilities for free. This theory can apply to lots of jobs that involve activities you enjoy: working at a nursery if you enjoy gardening; working as an usher if you love the theater; working as a tour guide at your favorite museum; etcetera.

- **Perks.** When you're a poor college student, perks definitely count. Maybe you can work at your favorite clothing store and get a discount, work at a movie theater and get free tickets, or work at a restaurant and get some good free meals.

The Resume Punch: Looking for a TKO

Sometimes people take jobs for reasons other than money. Yes, we know that this sounds like a ridiculous concept, but it may be the right thing for you to do.

Some jobs have what many people refer to as "resume punch." What they mean is that when a potential employer or graduate school looks at your resume, there is something so unique about your job experience that it literally jumps off the page. For example, if you were employed as the assistant to the United States Attorney General, that would have major league resume punch, no matter what you got paid. Similarly, if your resume indicated that you had spent three years helping research a cure for the AIDS virus, you'd be in good shape in your interview. In short, you need resume punch to separate you from the crowd of people being interviewed.

So how do you get one of these jobs? After all, not everyone can be the unpaid speech writer for the Queen of England. Actually, it's not quite that hard. You have two things going for you. First, since you're a college student, potential employers will see you as an educated resource they can plunder. The reason they can get away with this is the second thing you having going for you: since you're looking for experience, you'll work for free. Every employer likes the combination of a young, hard-working individual, striving to get a higher education, who will work for free.

You've got the package to get a job with resume punch; now you need to know where to look. In large part this depends on the field you're interested in. If you're interested in politics, see your representatives; if you're interested in social services, check out your local hospitals; if you're interested in business, see what you might do for a branch office of one of the brokerage houses. You must take the initiative to go out and get these jobs. The career placement office will not have them posted. Make your own opportunities!

Having said that, there are some employers who offer internships to college students. An internship is a type of structured volunteer work designed to give college students an opportunity to learn, firsthand, the facets of a particular field while giving the employer some much needed help. For example, the summer after his second year in college, Joe worked as an intern in the office of his local congresswoman. The work he did was far from glamorous, but he got an excellent idea of how a congressional office is run. Moreover, when the congresswoman ran for re-election, Joe was able to parlay his internship experience the year before into a full-time paid position on her campaign staff. To show you how these things snowball, Joe then worked full time on the congresswoman's legislative staff, and the next summer he was asked to work as a political consultant for the upcoming state elections based on his past experience.

Admittedly, internship opportunities are not easy to come by. As you might expect, since they've got good resume punch, many students are looking for internships. However, with the help of your school's career placement office, you should pursue internship opportunities. As in Joe's case, they can be well worth the effort.

Use Your Vacations Wisely

One question that always kills unsuspecting college students in interviews is: "Tell me what you were doing for the periods of time not listed on your resume." If your answer is that you were fly fishing in Mexico, or relaxing at the beach, you've just lost yourself a job.

The key is to use your vacation time wisely. It isn't important what you do during this time as long as you're doing something worthwhile. Now, don't get us wrong. We don't mean that over President's Day weekend or even spring break that you should be out volunteering your time. (Although Habitat for Humanity is a cool thing with resume punch to get involved with over spring break.) Instead, we're talking about the weeks off you have between your first and second semester each year, and over the summer.

No employer wants to hire someone who didn't take the initiative to do something over the summer. Moreover, they're never going to buy the line that there was nothing that was really in your field for you to do, so you played golf instead. Employers have a lot more respect for the person who admits that they worked waiting tables to make money to buy books.

You may get the best of both worlds by finding a job that you like as much as prospective employers do. One friend of ours taught tennis in Switzerland for a summer (not too shabby). He got to travel and have a great time, and employers loved his stories about trying to communicate concepts like forehand and backhand to non-English-speaking students. Despite nightmarish memories of herding bratty campers around as a camp counselor during high school, another friend decided to take a job teaching Hebrew the summer after her freshman year. Not only did this help pay the bills and look good on her resume, but it turned out to be a fantastic experience for her, one that opened up new interests and possibilities for the future. The moral of these stories?

No matter what you do, don't waste your vacation time.

A Final Note About Working

Working while you're in school can be valuable for reasons that reach far beyond your paychecks. We've already told you that jobs give you resume punch, but they can also help you figure out what you'll need that resume for. College jobs are a great way to try out different career possibilities. What better way to find out if you're majoring in the right subject and gearing up for the right career? Even if you can't get a job during school that specifically relates to your chosen field, you'll learn a lot about your employment preferences and abilities. Do you like working with people? Are you a good manager? Do you like to work on one long-term project or several short term tasks? How well do you handle pressure? These are all important things that can only be learned from experience. Other good reasons for working while you're in school? Mom and Dad will respect you for it. You'll get the satisfaction of providing yourself with the things you need and want. When you graduate, you'll enter the job market with more confidence and experience. And someday you can tell your college-age kids how hard you worked when you were in school.

CHAPTER 9

To Your Health

TAKE CARE OF YOURSELF

With all of the stuff you're expecting from your body, from studying all night to partying all night, it's more important than ever that you take good care of the old body. You're the only person who will know if you're eating your five fruits and vegetables a day, which means it may be more like five a month, and that's assuming popcorn counts as a vegetable. We know your freshman year lifestyle isn't likely to put you in the running for American Heart Association poster child, but we do want you to devote enough energy to your health to prevent illness and burnout. Do yourself (and your worried parents) a favor, and at least skim through this chapter.

GET SOME SLEEP

One of the negative things about being in a new place with tons of stuff to do is that there doesn't seem to be enough time in the day to do everything. To do everything, something has got to give. For most college students the thing that gives sooner or later is sleep.

"Not I," you say. "I slept until 2:30 in the afternoon on any day I didn't have to go to school, and sometimes when I did!" That mentality is about to change for several reasons. Most importantly, you'll want to be out doing things on campus. There are parties, shows, movies, lectures, and other events (including class) that will interest you enough that you'll force yourself to shower before noon. Moreover, you'll feel the college pressure that keeps students up studying till daybreak or waking up when it's still dark outside. When you have a chem exam the next day and you're still wondering why the periodic table of the elements bothers you every day, you'll put in extra hours.

Burning the candle at both ends occasionally won't kill you. In real life it happens to all of us. However, if you let it become a pattern you'll get seriously burnt out. Adults need an average of eight hours of sleep a night. That's an *average*. You can get less sometimes, but if you skimp too often, your body will demand some payback.

Trust us, sleep deprivation is an ugly thing. Generally, you don't even know how your performance is being affected. That's because lack of sleep tends to make you less cogent. Your thinking is slower and less effective when you haven't slept. The problem gets worse and worse as you continue to keep yourself up for too many hours.

Sometimes a combination of too little sleep, too much stress, and keeping strange hours develops into a serious problem: insomnia. Melanie, for instance, decided during her second semester freshman year that she didn't need to sleep anymore. Okay, she didn't consciously decide not to sleep, but she did get involved with so many activities that sleep slipped further and further down the list of priorities. The clincher was that she got cast in a play, which was great, but it opened the week after mid-terms, which wasn't so great. The week that she had all of the dress and technical rehearsals every night was also the week she had two papers due and three exams. Well, Mel decided she wasn't going to panic. When her day of classes and rehearsal finally ended around 10:30 or 11:00, she would grab a Coke and start writing or studying. Around 3:00 or 3:30 a.m., she would finally try to go to bed. The only problem was that by that point her mind felt like it had been stuck in a blender with a script, an anthropology text book, and a case of Diet Coke. Sleep usually arrived about twenty minutes before the alarm went off in the morning. A couple large coffees later, Mel was on her way through another day. The good news is that the play was great, the exams went fine, and the papers were handed in. The bad news is that after the week passed, the screwy sleeping habits wouldn't go away; and for two or three months Melanie struggled to get to sleep every night.

We're not saying that you'll become an insomniac if you pull a couple of all-nighters. However, it's never a good idea to force yourself into an unnatural sleeping pattern. It's a particularly bad idea to start relying on caffeine to give you the energy that you should be getting from sleep. If you do find that you're having trouble sleeping, we have a few suggestions:

- Don't do your work on your bed. Make sure your mind associates your pillow with sleep, not studying.

- Try to get up at about the same time every morning. It's tempting to sleep late to make up for your inability to fall asleep at night, but sleeping through the morning will further upset your internal clock, not to mention make you miss your morning classes.

- Hide the face of your alarm clock. Watching the minutes tick away while you're trying to fall asleep is infuriating.

- In another move to help you avoid frustration, don't force yourself to stay in bed if you just can't fall asleep. Get up and read a book or watch some stupid TV until you feel calm and sleepy enough to try again.

- No caffeine after noon.

- A couple hours before you go to bed, make a list of all of the things you have to do the next day. Tell yourself that once it's on the list, you don't have to worry about it any more until morning.

- Get some exercise every day. This is what finally cured Melanie's insomnia. Regular exercise is a great stress reliever *and* it tires your body out, making it easier to sleep. It may be especially helpful to work out three or four hours before you want to go to sleep. As your heart rate and body temperature drop after a workout you naturally feel sleepy.

- *Don't* take sleeping pills. These are not a solution. Before you know it, what was supposed to be a one-night solution becomes the only way you can sleep. Worse, if you take them too often, the recommended dose won't do anything for you anymore. A *bad idea*. If you want something to help you sleep, consider chamomile tea, milk, or bananas, all foods that are naturally soothing and encourage sleep.

- Know that you are not the only person awake at 3 a.m. Sometimes the worst part of not sleeping is feeling like everyone else is slumbering peacefully. Rest assured that there are other people out there with the same problem. It won't help you sleep, but it might make you feel a little better.

If you try our suggestions and you're still not sleeping, you should visit the campus health center. Sometimes insomnia is a symptom of another health problem, so you shouldn't ignore it if it persists. Insomnia can also be caused by depression or extreme stress, both of which you should seek outside help for. Doctors who work on campus are familiar with the plight of the sleepless, and will probably be very helpful.

EXERCISE

We mentioned that exercise can be a cure for insomnia, but it can be a cure for a lot more than that. Regular exercise will relieve stress, help you sleep, keep you from gaining the dreaded "freshman fifteen," and just generally make you a healthier, happier person. Plus, as you'll discover later in life, your college schedule is one of the most conducive to exercise that you'll ever have. That's because you usually have a free hour or two at some point during the day. You also have the bonus of your school's athletic facilities, and maybe even a campus that's good for running or walking.

How you want to get your exercise is up to you. It can be a great way to meet people if you join an intramural sports team, play Ultimate Frisbee, or take an aerobics class on campus. Conversely, exercise can be a great escape. Going for a nice long jog or popping your headphones on to ride an exercise bike can give you some uninterrupted thinking time. One note of caution here: Use your common sense when you exercise alone. Don't run alone if you don't know how safe a neighborhood is; and *definitely* don't run alone at night. Who knows? You may even be able to get credits for exercising. Tennis, karate, golf, cardiovascular fitness—you name it, there will be colleges that offer courses in it.

Think about all your body puts up with from you. From not enough sleep to too much pizza, it takes a lot of abuse. A little exercise will help balance the scales (literally). So make time for it. And, as Nike would say, Just Do It.

FOOD FOR THOUGHT

Pizza, beer, Doritos, Malomars, beer, Twinkies, beer, chocolate, beer, and beer are all foods that college students are fond of. In many cases, this is a direct response to the God-awful quality of the food being served by the dining services. Other times it's because college students like, well, you know, beer. Either way, you need to put the right stuff in your body in order to get the best stuff from it.

The freedom of college brings lots of people lots of things. For many, it brings relief from the pressure of mom and dad telling you what you can and cannot eat. (Liver and spinach= good, a box of Entenmann's chocolate chip cookies for dinner = bad.) As a result, many students come to college and start putting as much junk in their bodies as they can find. This is not a good idea.

As soon as you arrive on campus, you should begin to develop the routines that you will maintain for rest of your college career. As we've said, regular exercise and sleep are two important routines to establish. Healthy eating habits are also good to develop. There are several options students have when choosing how to feed themselves while in school. Typically, these include the campus dining service, using a kitchen in the dorm, making food in their rooms, and eating take-out food. It's probably a combination of these three ways of eating that will work best for you.

The key thing is to make sure you maintain a balanced diet. Have a salad at the dining hall, make some pasta a couple of nights a week, even have a frozen burrito or two. Just don't overdo the fatty foods, beer, and sugar. You've undoubtedly heard about the "freshman fifteen." It's not uncommon for first-year students to gain some weight, during their first semester especially. However, it doesn't have to be that way. College naturally presents you with an active lifestyle. In short, this means that since you're already burning more calories, a few Mars bars aren't going to kill you. Joe's father always used to tell him, "Everything in moderation, Joseph." The concept is important here.

Campus dining services are notorious for the average quality of their food. However, you probably don't need Julia Child as the head chef in order to survive college. The dining service usually offers three meals a day. At breakfast, you'll get your standard fare of eggs, pancakes, and the like. You'll probably also have a cereal bar. We love the cereal bar. It's the best thing about the dining service. You can have the Fruit Loops once in a while, but concentrate on the Wheaties or Cheerios. At lunch, you'll usually have at least one hot option, a soup perhaps, and a sandwich bar. Pretty much what you'd expect. Dinner is the kicker. You may have to scrounge a little here. The hot options can be revolting. You know, black stuff in a brown sauce with yellow rice. However, you might get lucky with a salad bar. The salad bar is the second best thing about the dining service. It's fresh and easy to prepare. Plus, you'll find that you miss vegetables after ignoring them for a good month or so.

Here are some tips for healthy eating:

- Don't linger over your meals with your friends; you'll just eat more than you really wanted. If you want to hang out for a while, make yourself a cup of tea, and keep both hands on your mug. It will help defeat the munchies.

- Don't always take dessert even if it seems to be the only edible thing offered. Check out the salad bar again. Or head to a local supermarket or deli and check out their salad bar. If you're a dessert addict, frozen yogurt is a good alternative. We used to stick Rice Krispies and marshmallows in a bowl in the microwave to make our extremely simplified version of the bars Mom used to make. It's messy and high in sugar, but at least it's low in fat.

- Don't cut out sweets entirely. Allow yourself a moderate amount of junk; otherwise, you'll end up wolfing down forbidden food one night. Make junk food a healthy part of your diet.

- Drink lots of water. You're running all over campus; your body fluids need replenishing frequently. Choose water instead of soda at meals; it has far fewer calories and sugar. It's clean (in most of the United States, at any rate); it's healthy.

These days more and more dining services, recognizing their weak past performance, have come up with new and exciting ideas for keeping the animals fed. For example, at NYU, a Burger King and a Pizza Hut accept your meal card as payment. We understand that at other schools, sub shops, pizza places, and other similar fast food restaurants do the same thing. These can bail you out in a jam, but don't make a Whopper or a slice your regular meal.

As we mentioned, you're also likely to find that you have a kitchen in your dorm for all residents to use. Although the kitchen is usually filthy, you can help yourself avoid the freshman fifteen by doing some of your own cooking. We're not talking Beef Wellington here. We mean, for example, pasta. Pasta will be the staple of your life at some point in college. And just when you've had enough of it, you'll graduate and eat it non-stop for a couple of years. But that's another book. Macaroni and cheese is a biggie. And don't forget Ramen. Cinnamon toast is also a possibility. We've heard that broccoli with salsa heated in the microwave is good. And there are lots of frozen foods that can be heated in a dorm kitchen. Cooking in the dorm can save you some money, while assuring that you recognize what's steaming in front of you.

There are a few brave souls who rely on their strictly illegal hot plate or microwave to eat in college. Don't be one of them. Besides braving a huge fine for having these appliances (they violate every fire code known to man), you won't have many eating options. While we won't deny that you can make soup and other things in your room that can serve as snacks or meals, after you've eaten your fiftieth frozen burrito, you'll be ready for something leafy and green. Besides, the dorm kitchen usually has facilities for making quick snacks or meals.

Your last option is to eat out all the time. We don't recommend this. While you may have a different wonderful and exotic meal every night, or even just take-out Chinese, you will go broke very quickly this way. Eat out on special occasions, Saturday nights, or when you really can't stand the sight of the dining services food (even the salad bar) for one more night.

CAMPUS HEALTH SERVICES

Add up bad eating habits, late nights, crazy schedules, shared bathrooms (read: germs), and a lack of exercise (if you didn't take our advice) and what do you get? Sick. Even if you do try to maintain a relatively healthy lifestyle you're going to get sick at some point. Unless your college is in your home town, it's not likely that Mom and Dad are going to pop by with aspirin and chicken soup. And although your roommate loves you (or not), she's got her own crazy schedule that keeps her from her duties as the Florence Nightingale of the dorms. Before you succumb to thoughts of starving to death because you can't drag your sick self to the cafeteria, remember that you are not alone. You have the campus health center.

We talked a little about the campus health center when we lectured you about safe sex. But handing out condoms and prescribing birth control pills is only the tip of the iceberg of what's offered at the health center. The centers at most colleges are staffed by nurses twenty-four hours a day, and always have a doctor on call. If you are running a fever, throwing up, or sprain your ankle at soccer practice, there's always someone around to take care of you. You can also schedule doctor's appointments to get an annual physical, ask about those headaches you've been having, any other health problem that's bothering you. Psychological counseling is also provided by most campus health services, which makes them the place to go if the stress is getting to you, you're not sleeping, or you're seriously contemplating lighting a bonfire with your roommate's clothes. The campus doctor can also issue prescriptions, and some campus centers have their own pharmacy.

Check it out when you're filling out all of your paperwork before you start school; school medical insurance is probably among the many things you're shelling out cash for. It's probably a good idea to pay the health services fee even if it's optional. Being able to pop into the clinic on campus can save you a lot of time and money. If you wake up with conjunctivitis (pink eye) or get a nasty sunburn lying out on the roof of the dorm, it's nice to be able to walk across campus and get the care you need. You may have heard that the health care offered on campus is not always the best. The truth is, you probably do want to go to your own doctor or the local hospital if there's a serious problem. However, from Band-Aids to condoms, the campus health care center can be a great resource.

CAMPUS SECURITY

The world is a dangerous place. This is unfortunate, but it's reality. Like anywhere else, on a college campus you need to be aware of the potential dangers and take caution to avoid them.

The amount of caution you need to take in avoiding unwelcome circumstances on campus will largely depend on where your campus is located. As you might expect, a major city campus may have more (and will certainly have different) types of potential security pitfalls than a small rural campus. Being aware of you're surroundings is important. It's easy to feel comfortable on your familiar college campus, and that's good. However, you don't want to let your guard down. Your campus security service can't possibly deter every potential threat to the student body. Even the Secret Service can't do that for the President. You must take some measures to protect yourself. Here are a few:

- **Lock Your Dorm Room:** Whether you're home or not, always be sure to lock your dorm room. When you're out there's always the potential for some criminal moron to come into your room and take your clothing, jewelry, money, etc. Theft on campus is not some rare occurrence. It happens all the time. Don't make a thief's job easier by leaving the door open. When you're in your room lock your door, too. We won't get into a list of potential crimes that can arise from an open door. You get the picture.

- **Use the Buddy System:** Yeah, we know this is kind of silly, but it is safe. Whether you're out jogging, studying, walking around campus late, going to a party or going off campus, it makes sense to have a partner. He or she can make sure you get home safe and get help if necessary. There's strength in numbers. We suppose that it's appropriate to note here that this is most appropriate for nighttime activities. Nonetheless, if there's not going to be anyone around, in the early morning, for example, bring a buddy.

- **Don't Give Out Your Address, Phone Number or Keys to Anyone You Don't Know**: This is such basic advice, but somehow people always forget it. A student meets someone else on campus and gives them their address and phone number on some pretext. The next thing they know they've got some weirdo who's keeps calling asking them if they want to go to dinner every night. Limit the information you give out about you, and you'll avoid such problems.

- **Act Like a Grown Up**: Don't abuse alcohol. Walk away from fights. Don't get caught up in the peer pressure to do stupid things. College is, in part, about having fun. You don't need to put yourself or others in danger to have fun.

In addition to these general tips, you should adopt your own safety strategy based on where you are going to school and your particular circumstances. Whatever the case, make sure that you're aware of your surroundings and prepared to avoid potential problems.

In Conclusion

You've read our book. Now you are completely prepared to take on every new experience your freshman year will offer, and come through it all with poise and great success. In fact, you'll probably be the most popular, academically successful, well-adjusted student that's ever entered college. Okay, maybe we're exaggerating, but not by much. You were headed for success long before we came on the scene. We know you won't remember everything we've written. Heck, you probably didn't even read it all. And that's just fine with us. What we really hope you take from our book is something far less specific than any one piece of advice. Nothing substitutes for personal experience, but reading about our experiences and those of our friends may at least take some of the anxiety out of your first days and weeks on campus.

As we said in our introduction, you are about to enter one of the most exciting times of your life. As our parting words, we encourage you to do it with vigor, enthusiasm, a reasonable degree of caution, and a bright outlook. We'll tell you now one thing you're likely to hear from anyone who's been to college: Enjoy it now, because it'll be over before you know it.

Best of luck to you.

—Mel and Joe

About the Authors

Melanie Sponholz graduated *summa cum laude* from Drew University in 1993. She started as an intern at Random House in 1992 and now works there as a Publishing Administrator. Mel enjoys running, reading, and traveling.

Joseph C. Sponholz graduated, *cum laude*, from New York University in 1994. He is a law student at Fordham University School of Law. He enjoys golf, skiing, and spending time with his beautiful wife.

Mel and Joe were married in 1995 and now live in New York.

Notes

Notes

Notes

Notes

Notes

Notes

Notes

Notes

Notes

Notes

Notes